Growing Woodland Plants

Growing
Woodland Plants

Clarence and Eleanor G. Birdseye

DOVER PUBLICATIONS, INC.
NEW YORK

International Standard Book Number: 0-486-20661-0
Library of Congress Catalog Card Number: 72-87872

Manufactured in the United States of America
Dover Publications, Inc.
180 Varick Street
New York, N.Y. 10014

Preface

The purpose of *Growing Woodland Plants* is to teach both novices and experienced gardeners to recognize, enjoy, conserve, cultivate, and propagate, on any desired scale, approximately 200 species of wildflowers and ferns native to our American woodlands. Emphasis is placed on species occurring principally north of Virginia and east of Montana, because the authors have gained their experience in that area and also because space prohibits inclusion of all American woods plants. Nevertheless, the instructions are applicable wherever woods-wildflowers can be grown. Only everyday language that can be readily understood by beginners is used. Confusing technical words are conspicuous by their scarcity; but there is a glossary explaining the few unusual words that are employed.

Successful cultivation of woodland plants need be neither complex nor expensive; even a small woodsgarden can yield big dividends in pleasure, knowledge, and health. What is more, the work involved need not be too strenuous, even for older people.

The propagation of woodland plants, conscientiously carried out, can do much to preserve, and even increase, the supply of native wildflowers, many of which are already extremely scarce. Many kinds of flowers and ferns multiply rapidly under cultivation and soon furnish a substantial surplus, which can be reintroduced to suitable uncultivated areas. This hobby, therefore, can be made an aid to, rather than an enemy of, true conservation.

Do not follow the suggestions in this book slavishly, even though they are both detailed and simple. Wildflower gardening is an art as well as a science, and its practice permits of almost infinite variety and initiative. Let Nature be your teacher. The woods themselves are the places to learn a thousand and one interesting and important facts about their inhabitants. So wherever you find wildflowers growing luxuriantly, observe the conditions of terrain, soil, light, groundcover, and associations under which they flourish. Then mix your knowledge with imagination—and apply both to your garden.

That wildflower gardening can become a fascinating hobby even for those who have never before been at all interested in small woods plants is indicated by the casual way in which we ourselves got started.

As a youngster, I—the not-so-senior author—spent twenty-five years as field naturalist, hunter, trapper, and fur-trader in the deserts, mountains, woods, and tundras of North America from Mexico to Labrador. During those years I came to know scientifically and intimately most of this continent's mammals, birds, reptiles, and trees, but I had absolutely no interest in small plants; during that quarter-century, I tramped and rode unnoticing over hundreds of miles of wildflowers and ferns.

Then we moved to Gloucester, Massachusetts, and Eleanor joined a garden club. Soon she began identifying wildflowers and ferns of which I knew nothing. That was bad for family discipline—for *I* was supposed to be the naturalist of the clan. About that time, too, a gale wrecked my forty-foot offshore fishing boat and abruptly ended my hobby of placing migration markers in sixty-foot, fifty-ton finback whales. Simultaneously, a developing case of angina pectoris imperiously suggested a less strenuous form of outdoor recreation.

So, suddenly and completely, I ceased to be a horny-handed harpooner and became a babysitter for the gentle maidenhair and dainty ladyslipper. Whale hunting, though exciting, must necessarily be taken, by a businessman, in small doses and limited areas. But wildflowers and ferns can be found in every field and along every country road and can be propagated almost anywhere in spare time. More important, while seasickness had kept Eleanor from joining me in whaling, we have been able to pursue our wildflower hobby together for a score of years.

Growing Woodland Plants consists of two parts. In Part 1, we have discussed in detail some basic characteristics of woodlands in relation to wildflower gardening; the preparation and care of woodsgardens; the collection and propagation of flowers and ferns; the utilization of surplus plants; and winter-forcing. Part II contains detailed descriptions and cultural directions for more than 200 kinds of wildflowers and ferns desirable for woodsgardens.

Plant Names

In this book every plant is referred to by one or more popular names and its scientific name. There is little agreement among botanists regarding either type of appellation; but one widely accepted authority on both is *Standardized Plant Names,* prepared for the American Joint Committee on Horticultural Nomenclature by Harlan P. Kelsey and William A. Dayton and printed by J. Horace McFarland Company of Harrisburg, Pennsylvania. We have followed *Standardized Plant Names* exactly for scientific names; but, in order that our readers may more readily recognize their old wildflower friends, we have added many well-known popular names to those approved by Kelsey and Dayton. In many cases, also, we have reinserted hyphens omitted by *Standardized Plant Names.*

Clarence Birdseye

Gloucester, Massachusetts
January 1951

NOTE: It is strongly recommended that you become familiar with local ordinances, which in some instances forbid the removal from the natural environment of certain species.

Acknowledgments

Because the authors do not consider themselves 'authorities' on much of anything horticultural, they have consulted numerous authoritative books and have submitted appropriate portions of the manuscript to friends of national reputation in their several fields. Many helpful criticisms have been received and incorporated in the text; and, as a result, the authors are confident that *Growing Woodland Plants* is scientifically sound, although couched in layman's language. Among those who have been most helpful are:

Professors R. O. Holdsworth and Arnold D. Rhodes, Forestry Dept., University of Massachusetts, Amherst, Mass.

Harlan P. Kelsey, East Boxford, Mass.

Dr. Elmer D. Merrill, Arnold Arboretum, Boston, Mass.

Mr. Harold S. Ross, President of Boston Horticultural Club, Boston, Mass.

Mr. E. L. D. Seymour, Horticultural Editor, *The American Home.*

Dr. Edgar T. Wherry, Professor of Botany, University of Pennsylvania.

Dr. Donald Wyman, Arnold Arboretum, Boston, Mass.

Contents

PART ONE

I   *Woodland Conditions*

Woodland plants have through untold thousands of years become adapted to life under practically every kind of forest environment. But each species of plant has fitted itself to flourish most luxuriantly in some particular kind of surroundings. Therefore, if a woodland gardener wishes to cultivate successfully a broad cross section of northern wildflowers and ferns, he must reproduce in his garden acceptable imitations of several types of forest conditions.

Of course any forest is the result of the interaction of an almost unlimited number of factors, principal among which are altitude, latitude, slope exposure, direction of prevailing winds, rainfall, humidity, temperature, drainage, topography, subsoil, surface and sub-surface rock formations, soil acidity, and amount of sunlight.

The kinds of trees composing any given forest are largely determined by the prevailing combination of the factors above, for each species of tree flourishes best under a relatively narrow range of conditions. But, although trees are the creatures of their environment, they themselves create a variety of habitats, each of which has its appropriate association of lesser plants. For instance, a grove of white pines provides such dense year-round shade, so impervious a cover of needles, and such strongly acid needlemold that the forest floor may be almost bare of small plants. An oak forest, on the other hand, has no winter shade at all, allows early spring sunshine to warm the ground, provides a well-aerated groundlitter of leaves, and has a somewhat less strongly acid humus-rich soil. Most maples provide still another set of conditions, for the soil under them is usually neutral or only slightly acid. In a mixed hemlock-pine-oak-beech forest, there is a thin layer of strongly acid humus-rich soil, ample winter sunlight, and at least some sunny spots even in the summer.

Except where man or fire has interrupted nature's processes, woods soil consists of the same intergrading layers. On the

[3]

very top is a groundlitter of fallen needles, leaves, twigs, branches, prone tree trunks, and other debris. As more and more material is added on the upper side of this layer, the organic matter near its underpart gradually decomposes and merges into the second layer—leafmold that is practically pure partially decayed vegetable matter known as humus.

But considerable mineral matter, too, gets added to the soil. Flooded streams spread gravel and sand. Winds drop inorganic dust onto the forest floor. Birds, mammals, and insects die and contribute their share of mineral matter. Leaves, twigs, and other vegetation decompose and return to the soil minerals picked up by the roots of growing plants. Rocks are split by frost and roots into boulders and stones; and these are fined down to gravel and sand by repeated temperature changes, small animals, and chemical reactions.

Gradually the inorganic material thus added to the surface of the forest floor works downward through the litter and humus layers and accumulates into a subsoil, or third layer, which contains less and less vegetable and more and more mineral matter from its upper to its lower portions. Lastly, under this subsoil there lies solid rock or clay-like hardpan containing practically no humus at all. But even this basic layer is not unchanging, for a sort of chemical digestion of rocks and other inorganic material takes place below the forest floor, and its products work upward into the subsoil and, by many and devious routes, even into the humus itself.

Although this general soil pattern holds for practically all types of woodlands, there may be literally dozens of variations in a single acre. For instance, the depth of the humus layer may vary from a fraction of an inch to more than a foot; the acidity of the soil under a small group of hemlocks will be much greater than that under near-by basswoods or poplars; an adjacent area may be closely boulder-strewn; groundlitter and rich humus may be entirely lacking where fire has raged; there may be standing water in a low spot with clay subsoil; a flooding brook may have covered a few near-by square yards with sand; and, rising above these lower areas, a granite ledge may offer precarious root-holds for everything from ladyslippers to a gnarled old oak. But although these varied habitats are close together, each will shelter its own congenial group of plants which could not flourish under markedly different conditions.

SOIL ACIDITY

The chemical characteristics of the forest floor are key factors in the life of every woods plant, from micro-organism to tree; and soil acidity is one of the most important. So let us consider briefly and in a nontechnical way just what soil acidity is, how it is created under natural conditions, means for measuring it, and in what manner it can be regulated in your garden.

Soil may be alkaline, neutral, or acid. This may be clearer to you if you remember that such materials as household ammonia and baking soda are alkaline, while orange juice and vinegar are acid. If one of these alkalis is mixed in the right proportion with one of the acids, the resulting mixture will be neutral—that is, there will be no preponderance of either alkali or acid.

The degree of soil alkalinity or acidity is stated in terms of its pH—which is merely a convenient unit of measurement like pounds or inches. *Very acid* soils have the lowest numbers on the pH scale, and for the purposes of this book are rated from pH 4 to 5. *Moderately acid* ones may be anywhere from pH 5 to 6. *Slightly acid* soils are from pH 6.0 to 6.9. Neutral materials—those that are neither acid nor alkaline—register pH 7; and our most alkaline woodland soils seldom are higher than pH 7.5. The degree of acidity or alkalinity in a soil is known as its 'reaction,' just as the measurement of that reaction is its pH number. For example, the *reaction* of the soil around your pink ladyslipper is probably very acid—about pH 4.5; if you have recently tested the *reaction* of your compost pile, you will probably find it averages about pH 5.5 to 6.0.

Simple and inexpensive methods of measuring soil pH are described in this chapter, in the section on 'Soil Testing.'

Some factors that tend to make woods soils acid are decaying vegetable matter, decomposing granite, water that has been acidified by contact with such materials, and removal of alkaline substances from the soil by plants. Important factors tending to neutralize acid soils are water-borne alkalis dissolved out of subsoils and such rocks as limestone, alkaline material re-

[5]

turned to the soil by the decomposition of forest plants, and the action of earthworms and other animals that carry soil upward from the lower levels.

At any rate, interaction of these and many other factors determines whether any given soil is alkaline, neutral, or acid. Almost none of our northern forest soils are more than slightly alkaline; only a very few are approximately neutral; many are slightly or moderately acid; and the rest are quite strongly so.

Acidity is usually greatest near the surface, where decomposing, acid-containing plant matter constantly replenishes the supply, and is less in the underlying layers of soil and subsoil, where alkaline substances from the hardpan or underlying rock may tend to neutralize or counteract the acid derived from leaf-mold.

Another reason for differing degrees of soil acidity is that some kinds of living vegetation contain much more acid than others, and when these plants decompose they impart differing percentages of acid to the resulting humus. Most coniferous trees are relatively rich in acid-forming materials, and their needles when decomposed make strongly acid soil. Leaves of oak, beech, blueberry, rhododendron, azalea, and laurel also contain much acid, which they impart to the soil. Cedar, basswood, hickory, ash, and poplar generate only very slightly acid humus.

Water is another powerful chemical agent, for it, too, may be acid, neutral, or alkaline. For instance, if very acid drainage from a sphagnum bog flows underground for a distance and then emerges still acid from a woodland spring, the soil around that spring may be ideal for acid-loving plants; but if the bed of the streamlet leading from the spring is of limestone, the water will soon become neutral or even alkaline and in its new condition may prove deadly to acid-loving vegetation.

Although some wildflowers and ferns are tolerant of varying degrees of soil acidity, other species have little or no such tolerance. For example, wild geraniums and great solomonseal are among the tolerant plants, while pink ladyslippers and trailing arbutus simply must have very acid soil. Therefore, the soil of your woodsgarden must be not only humus-rich but of suitable acid content for all of the plants you may wish to grow in it. This requirement is not difficult to meet: when

[6]

you start your garden, simply make all the soil moderately acid (pH 5–6), which will do very nicely for a majority of your plants. Then alter the acidity of limited areas to meet the requirements of the acid-intolerant species. That, too, is easy (see pp. 31–32).

Micro-Organisms of the Soil

The tiny bacteria and fungi that inhabit forest soil are no less important than its chemical composition and its physical make-up. Without these microscopic plants there could be neither woods, nor wildflowers to live in them.

Micro-organisms play an essential part in transforming leaves and other groundlitter into humus. They aid, directly or indirectly, in decomposing solid rocks and gravel into loam and a great variety of essential plant foods. Some take nitrogen—which plants require as urgently as humans do oxygen—from the air and make it readily available. And they act as 'wet nurses' for orchids and a great many other plants by clustering about their roots and supplying them with nourishment they could not otherwise take up.

But don't let these biological facts of woods life dismay you, for every plant and every handful of leafmold brought from the woods to your compost pile or garden will carry its own bacteria and fungi, which will quickly spread through the 'synthetic' woods soil you have prepared.

Plant Foods

Wildflowers, like the garden varieties, must eat to live. Most plant food is derived from the soil and consists of several principal substances—nitrogen, phosphorus, potassium, calcium, iron, and magnesium—and a considerable number of minor, or 'trace,' elements such as copper and boron.

Good woodland soil is sufficiently rich in all these elements; and the synthetic soil you prepare for your garden will also contain ample plant food.

Soil Testing

Ordinary farm and garden soils should be tested frequently to determine such vital characteristics as acidity or alkalinity, content of both major and minor food elements, texture, and amount of organic matter (humus). But, because the 'synthetic' soil of your woodsgarden will surely be of good texture, rich in humus, and amply supplied with plant foods, you will usually need to test only for acidity. These acidity tests should, however, be made frequently, and should include all soils and soil ingredients used in connection with your gardening activities—e.g. needlemolds and leafmolds, woods soil collected with your plants, woods-compost, chemical solutions, and the soil used for propagating wildflowers from seeds and cuttings. Moreover, you will find it interesting to make a 'pH survey' of the area in which you hunt wildflowers—to study the reactions (pH) not only of soils but of ditch water, ponds, rivers, city tapwater, et cetera.

Fortunately, the use of indicator papers makes testing for soil reaction—acidity or alkalinity—so simple that anyone can do it successfully. These indicators are just strips of thin blotting paper treated with chemicals which always assume certain colors when wetted with water of given degrees of acidity or alkalinity. The wetted papers are then matched against accompanying color charts, each color representing a certain pH number.

The use of indicator papers for various purposes is extremely simple. In soil testing, a representative soil sample—about a heaping tablespoonful—is placed in a small glass or jar, and a little more than enough neutral (pH 7.0, made as suggested below) water slowly added to saturate the soil thoroughly without making it runny. Then the mixture is stirred with a spoon, heaped against the side of the glass, and allowed to stand until a few drops of water have drained into the bottom of the glass. Next, a short length of indicator paper is wetted with the water, and the changed color of the paper is matched against the color chart to determine the soil's pH number. It is as simple as that; and after a few trials you will be as skilled —for your own woodsgardening purposes—as any chemist in the land!

But although testing for soil reaction (pH) is very easily done, a few precautions are necessary. First, remember that contact with your hands may appreciably affect the reaction of a small quantity of soil, and that you should take your samples with a metal spoon, and keep them in glass containers such as jelly glasses or pint jars. Have in mind, too, that soil is not of uniform reaction (pH) over any considerable area or at different depths, and that several small samples, each consisting of about a tablespoonful, should be combined to form a larger one from which the portion to be actually tested should be taken.

At times you will wish to test the pH (reaction) of water or of solutions made from chemical plant foods such as superphosphate, ammonium sulphate, and garden lime. To do so, simply dip the indicator paper in the solution and match the resultant color against the pH chart.

Only neutral (pH 7) water should, as we have already said, be used for making soil tests. To produce such water, nearly fill a pint jar with tapwater; determine its pH; if it is acid (below pH 7), bring it to neutral by adding a little baking soda; if alkaline (above pH 7), neutralize it with a little vinegar. Then keep it handy, and test it from time to time to check its reaction.

Indicator papers are, collectively, made to cover the whole pH range—numbers 1 to 14; and individual papers may be operable over many or only a few pH numbers. However, only the narrow-range papers—those that individually cover only 3 pH points or less—are sufficiently accurate for our purposes. They are made by several manufacturers under various trade names, but are usually obtainable only from chemical supply houses.

II   *Making Synthetic Soil*

Because very few wildflower gardens can be made entirely of rich woodland soil, the woodsgardener should learn how to prepare a synthetic soil that will meet all the requirements of woods plants. This can be done easily, inexpensively, and quickly.

Synthetic woodsgarden soil must be humus-rich, more or less acid, friable, well drained, uncompacted, inoculated with woodland types of bacteria and fungi, and as free as possible from the pests and diseases of domesticated plants. Such soil may be produced slowly in compost piles, or rapidly right on the site of your new garden; or it may be purchased from a commercial supplier..

COMPOST

Compost is a man-made, humus-rich mixture of mineral (inorganic) matter and decayed plant and animal (organic) material, and contains a much larger percentage of organic matter than is found in even the best garden loam.

Compost is to a woodsgardener what flour, sugar, and salt are to a good cook: neither gardener nor cook can produce satisfactory results without the right ingredients. Certainly no one who grows wildflowers should be without a good stock of compost, some 'in process,' and some ready for immediate use.

Compost is produced in piles ('heaps'), bins, or pits; and, since these are rather unsightly, they should be located in an inconspicuous spot. Moreover, compost piles must be kept constantly damp throughout and an ample water supply should therefore be conveniently available. The piles may be built in either sun or shade—preferably the former if they are frequently watered. Air, with its oxygen, must penetrate the pile, so do not make it too large or too compact.

Compost piles may be of any convenient shape, but at all times should have concave tops to catch water. Side walls are not absolutely necessary, but are very convenient; and we have found that ordinary galvanized 1-inch mesh chicken wire 36-inches wide makes excellent retaining walls. A 15½-foot length of such wire, ends brought together and fastened securely, will do nicely for a small circular pile about 5 feet in diameter. When the pile is to be moved, stirred, or used, these wire walls can be readily removed simply by unfastening their joined ends.

Organic Ingredients. Because fully 75 per cent of woods-garden compost should be organic matter and because the finished product must be definitely acid, the acidity of the various raw materials must be taken into consideration.

Strongly acid (about pH 4–5) organic materials include granulated peat and sphagnum moss; needles and needlemold of hemlock, spruce, fir, and pine; leaves and leafmold of oak, beech, chestnut, blueberry, huckleberry, laurel, azalea, and rhododendron; cranberry vines and living sphagnum moss; and shredded tobacco leaves and stems, cottonseed and castor-bean meal, and apple pomace.

Moderately acid (approximately pH 5–6) organic matter includes leaves and leafmold of red maple and most birches.

Slightly acid or neutral (pH 6–7) organic material includes lawn clippings, garden plants, saltmarsh reeds and hay, seaweed and corncobs (preferably ground); leaves of hickory, butternut, ash, most maples, elm, dogwood, poplar, basswood, willow, tulip-tree and many ornamental shrubs; and garbage and various sorts of animal manures.

In selecting the organic components of your compost pile use principally those materials having pH values below 6.0, and try to avoid anything that may be infected with plant diseases, pestiferous insects, or weed seeds. A large proportion of such pests would be killed during the composting process, but some would be sure to survive and add considerably to your future garden labors.

Inorganic Ingredients. Inorganic materials should constitute approximately 25 per cent of woodsgarden compost. These inorganic substances should consist principally of garden loam and minute quantities of certain chemicals that give added nutritive value, increase acidity, hasten decomposition, improve consistency, or otherwise make the compost more useful to woods plants.

[11]

Three valuable inorganic chemical ingredients of woodsgarden compost are powdered sulfur, superphosphate, and ammonium sulphate. Their use increases both the acid and nutritive content of woods soil. Only small quantities are needed; and all three may be purchased from farm- or garden-supply houses. Aluminum sulphate increases acidity without being nutritious.

Living Ingredients. Bacteria and fungi are essential elements of every good soil, for without them neither garden plants nor wildflowers can flourish. However, the kinds of micro-organisms found in ordinary domestic garden soil are not acid-tolerant and will not thrive in even moderately acid soil. Therefore, acid-tolerant species from the woods must be introduced to your woodsgarden compost. They abound in the humus under hemlock, white pine, beech, and oak trees, and humus from such locations should be added to your compost. Only small quantities are needed, and the necessary amounts—preferably from several different types of woods—may be easily obtained along the roadside.

Making a Compost Pile. Compost piles may be constructed in a great variety of ways, but one simple and entirely satisfactory procedure is as follows.

Select a location and set up chicken-wire retaining walls, leaving in place any low vegetation growing on the site. Spread over that vegetation about 4 inches of organic matter, at least two-thirds of which is of the strongly or moderately acid kinds. Add a ½-inch layer of garden soil and sprinkle on it ½ cupful each of superphosphate and powdered sulfur for each square yard of surface. Again build up a 4-inch layer of acid organic matter, preferably including about ¼ inch of cottonseed meal or soybean pomace. Then add another ½-inch layer of loam and sprinkle it with one cupful of ammonium sulphate. Next, with a garden fork, mix together all the material so far put into the pile. Keep on repeating approximately the foregoing steps until the pile is about one-half foot higher than the wire retaining walls. Top with a ½-inch layer of garden loam, and, finally, spread over the loam a paper-thin layer of aluminum or ammonium sulphate, or powdered sulfur to make the surface so acid that none but the most acid-resistant weeds can grow in it. Water each layer while the pile is accumulating,

[12]

and never let it become dry. But do not water so heavily that nutrient substances will be leached away.

A pile made in this way will be slow to decompose because the more acid the material, the more slowly decomposition will take place. Although many factors affect the time required for composts to ripen, you should plan to let yours remain in the pile for about one year. Meanwhile it should be thoroughly stirred for its full depth, or preferably transferred from one pile to another, about three times.

Compost made in the foregoing way will be of ideal texture, very high nutritive value, and moderately acid—pH 5–6. You will find innumerable uses for it in addition to those specifically suggested in this book. For a simple method of testing soil acidity see chapter 1, page 8.

Composting on the Garden Site

Although synthesizing your own woodsgarden soil via the compost pile is interesting, instructive, and inexpensive, and does not involve much hard work, it is a very slow process. Therefore, if you want to get a new garden started quickly, and have no ready-to-use compost available, proceed approximately as follows.

Remove from your garden site from 6 to 12 inches of soil, the depth depending on circumstances—e.g. how much digging you want to do and how far you are willing to have the surface of your garden rise above the surrounding area. On the bottom of the excavation place a 3-inch layer of equal parts of cottonseed or castor-bean meal and granulated peat. Then apply ⅛ inch of superphosphate and dig the whole layer well and deeply into the underlying soil. This will give you about an 8-inch layer of rich, porous, moderately acid subsoil. Water thoroughly, but not enough to make the mixture muddy.

Remove stones and roots from some of the excavated soil and spread about 5 inches of that soil over the newly prepared subsoil. Add a 4-inch layer of the organic materials listed above and top it off with ⅛ inch of superphosphate. Repeat the digging-in and stirring operations until the soil is of uniform composition. Water thoroughly.

Now add 1 inch of the original soil (or any at least fairly good garden loam), 2 inches of the organic materials, and a

[13]

paper-thin layer each of superphosphate and ammonium sulphate. Dig and mix this upper layer into the next lower one, and water as before. Spread on ½ inch, or more, of real woods humus, and a generous cover of groundlitter.

Allow the new garden to set for a month (if your patience holds out that long), pH-test the rich soil 2 inches under the groundlitter, and adjust the acidity of the several garden areas to the desired point. Set in your wildflowers and ferns—and you'll be started as a woodsgardener!

More detailed instructions for garden-making are given in chapter IV.

BUYING THE JOB

Perhaps you'll want a good nurseryman or landscape gardener to make your woodsgarden for you. He will be glad to do so, using his favorite materials for the job. But be sure that he uses plenty of humus and gets the soil sufficiently acid—about, on the average, pH 5–6. Make your own tests for soil acidity.

EARTHWORMS

Earthworms are highly desirable in slightly acid to neutral domestic soils (pH 6–7), but the common kinds do not thrive in even moderately acid woods soil. Therefore there is no use in adding them to your compost pile; and their presence there in large numbers is a sure indication that the pile is not sufficiently acid for most woodsplants. They may, however, be advantageously 'seeded' into the least acid (pH 6–7) areas of your woodsgarden.

III   *Stepping-Stones, Paths, and Groundlitter*

STEPPING-STONES

Wildflowers and ferns cannot thrive in compacted soil. A great many of them multiply principally by underground stems, which must be able to run freely through the loose leafmold just under the groundlitter. Therefore you should never permit anyone—including your own good self—to set foot on the ground of your garden. Instead, use stepping-stones at sufficiently frequent intervals to permit you to work everywhere in the garden without stepping on the ground. But don't make paths out of the stepping-stones, for that will destroy the illusion of woodsiness. Moreover, never use unweathered stones or stones of kinds incompatible with those which occur naturally in or near your garden area. For instance, don't use limestone rocks where granite abounds, for they just won't 'fit in' with the surroundings.

As a rule, you can't do better than to raid shaded old stone-walls for rocks of various sizes and interesting shapes, preferably flat below and rounded above. Select stones that are well spotted with lichens or moss. If you find rounded stepping-stones too 'teetery' for feet not as young as they used to be, flat stones may be laid on the surface and raised from year to year as decomposing groundlitter gradually builds up the surface level. A few interestingly deformed pieces of oak or hemlock firewood may be used to pinch-hit for stepping-stones. These logs—especially the hemlock ones—will quickly begin to decompose, and within two or three years may furnish ideal lodging for lichens, fungi, and the roots of such interesting creeping plants as goldthread, dwarf ginseng, and beadruby.

These numerous stepping-stones and chunks of wood will not lessen the number of plants your garden can support, for many wildflowers and ferns thrive best when nestled against a rock or log, and during the summer grow freely around and over it.

[15]

Paths

Paths are essential in any garden so large that all parts of it cannot be distinctly viewed from its borders. Moreover, the paths must be well defined—preferably with a combination of weathered logs and rocks—to keep your overenthusiastic guests within bounds.

Long paths should be winding and so arranged as to disclose choice plantings unexpectedly. To make the paths less conspicuous and more attractive, beadrubies, violets, oakferns, hepaticas, Dutchmans-breeches, and other low-growing species should be planted along their sides. Paths should be strewn deeply with needles or leaves for forest softness and to choke out weeds. In short, the paths should be as much as possible like woodland trails and will be one of the most delightful features of your garden.

Groundlitter

Every square foot of a normal forest floor is covered with needles, cones, pieces of bark, rotted tree boles, twigs, stumps, leaves, and other bits of debris, large and small. This groundlitter is the very basis of forest life, for it retards erosion, retains moisture, keeps the surface cool in summer and relatively warm in winter, provides suitable cover for germinating seeds and spreading rootstocks, and progressively decomposes to furnish the life-giving humus without which the myriad woodland plants could not become established and flourish.

Groundlitter is also an artistic necessity, for without it your garden cannot look 'woodsy.' Moreover, collecting it is fun, for almost every time you walk into the woods you can find some interesting piece of birchbark, a rotted branch, cones and acorns, a small moss-covered stump, a fallen tree fungus, or another lichen-rich stone of unusual shape. Woodland and ledge mosses and large fungi are themselves fascinating subjects for study and may well constitute an important aspect of a wildgarden. But they, like other plants, will flourish only under just the right combinations of moisture, light, soil reaction, and shade.

In short, your garden soil should be completely covered with the finer kinds of groundlitter and plentifully sprinkled with the larger odds and ends of forest debris.

IV   *Making the Woodsgarden*

Selecting the Site

There is no such thing as an 'ideal' site for a woodsgarden; and, anyway, most people have little choice. Fortunately, though, a thoroughly adequate garden can be created practically anywhere. Some very satisfactory locations are on the shady side of a wall, under a single big tree or a group of smaller ones, a shaded ledge, in the shelter of dense shrubbery, wood lots, and along forest paths. But in selecting your garden site, have in mind that no matter how small your first garden may be, constantly increasing enthusiasm will make you want to keep extending it.

Every woodsflower garden must have good drainage, ample shade, protection from wind, a convenient water supply, and freedom from intrusion of alkaline substances into the garden area.

The garden may be any size and shape, all in one area, or scattered around in numerous shady spots. Even if there isn't any shade immediately available, first temporary and then permanent shade means can be readily provided.

Excavating, and Providing Soil

For small gardens, the original soil should be excavated to a depth of 18 inches, unless ledge or hardpan intervenes, in which case the surface of the finished garden will be somewhat higher than the surrounding soil. As a matter of fact, a raised surface is desirable rather than otherwise.

As the earth is dug out, roots, even of valued shade trees, should be cut off and removed—so long as not more than about 20 per cent of the total roots of any one tree are severed. If you are in doubt on this matter, ask the advice of a nurseryman.

After excavation has been completed, place a 2-inch layer of crushed granite, cinders, or sharp sand in the bed to assure adequate drainage and to deter earthworms from carrying alkaline subsoil upward into your acid garden loam. If you are building your garden over a sloping or well-drained granite ledge, this drainage layer is not necessary; but if the garden surmounts a limestone or marble ledge, the drainage layer is important if acid-loving plants are to be grown.

If the garden is located where grass, weeds, and other undesirable growths are likely to encroach upon it, a 9-inch wide band of galvanized sheet metal, coated on both sides with a good tree paint (which can be purchased at any garden-supply store), should be buried with its upper edge just level with the soil of the surrounding area. A similar metal band should be used to prevent alkaline substances from entering the garden from any adjacent brick or concrete wall. In this latter case, the metal should be at least 2 inches away from the wall and the intervening space should be filled with crushed granite, cinders, or sand to permit seepage downward to the drainage layer, located under the garden.

Over the layer of drainage material, spread 6 inches of the excavated soil, or of any good garden loam; on top of that, sprinkle a ⅛-inch layer of equal parts of commercial superphosphate, ammonium sulphate, and powdered sulfur. This mixture of chemicals is an acid plant food that will counteract the alkaline content of the garden loam and help make it an ideal subsoil for a woodsgarden. These three fertilizers may be purchased from any farm- or garden-supply company. Mix the soil and the fertilizer thoroughly and water lightly.

Next, apply a 2-inch layer of garden loam and 2 inches of woods-compost, the latter prepared as directed in chapter 11. Spread on ½ inch of cottonseed meal or castor-bean pomace (also obtainable from a farm-supply house) and another ⅛-inch layer of the three chemicals. Again mix thoroughly and water adequately.

Now lay on 6 inches of compost, which, if rightly prepared, will have an acid value of about pH 5 to 6. If the pH number is lower than 5.0, add about 2 pounds of garden lime per 100 square feet to raise it slightly; or if the pH is above 6, sprinkle on 1 to 2 pounds of powdered sulfur and ammonium sulphate, mixed.

Thoroughly mix the compost and chemicals, and again water the garden well. Bound the garden with interestingly deformed cordwood, lichen-covered rocks, or weathered logs from the woods. Add stepping-stones, and paths if necessary. Spread on a generous layer of groundlitter. Let the soil settle for at least a few days, or as long as three weeks if that is convenient.

If your proposed garden is so large that the original soil cannot be easily removed, it may be partially excavated, spaded up, and enriched by dug-in materials, as suggested on pp. 13–14.

In a small garden, it is frequently desirable to grow in close proximity plants requiring very different degrees of soil acidity and moisture. For instance, you may want to grow pink, yellow, and showy ladyslippers all in one restricted area—yet these species will not all thrive in the same soil or with the same amount of water. In such a situation, a simple but effective procedure is to surround the area allotted to each kind of plant, or to each group of plants having the same cultural requirements, with 9-inch galvanized and painted sheet metal buried so that its upper edge is covered by the groundlitter. This method isolates each little patch of garden and permits appropriate care of its inhabitants.

PROVIDING SHADE

You are indeed fortunate if your new garden is already well shaded by a wall or by good-sized trees. But even if you had to dig it in a sunny spot and are depending temporarily on an arbor or canopy for shelter, you can soon create natural tree-shade in any one of several ways.

First, select the suitable varieties of trees you would most like to have. Among the best (because their needles and leaves decompose into acid humus) are hemlocks, pines, spruces, firs, beeches, and any of the oaks and birches. Avoid poplars, aspens, maples, hickories and walnuts, ash, cherries, cedars, and basswoods, for their leafmold is nearly neutral. However, perhaps not all of the desirable trees will thrive in your locality. Hemlocks, white pines, and firs, for instance, are not all suitable for areas buffeted by ocean winds and spray. So, before you begin your tree planting, get suggestions from a local nurseryman.

The least expensive, though slowest, way to get your shade

[19]

trees is to start them from seed you pick up from roadsides and woods. A few handfuls of assorted acorns will do the job nicely. Set them, soon after they fall to the ground, an inch below the surface in the garden or in similarly prepared spots around it, and protect from rodents for the first winter!

A somewhat quicker and equally inexpensive procedure is to transplant small wild seedlings from roadsides and woods, where you can always find oaks, birches, pines, beeches, hemlocks, and lots of others. If these are carefully transplanted in the late summer, early fall, or very early spring, they should grow from one to four feet annually.

If finances permit, larger trees can be purchased from your local nurseryman—who can even create a miniature forest for you over the weekend. For large gardens, quantities of small trees can usually be purchased for a nominal price from the State Forestry Department or other appropriate organization.

When you plant acorns or other tree seeds for quick shade, set them only a few inches apart. Not all of them will germinate; and if too many do sprout, you can easily cull out the excess. Likewise, if you transplant small trees into and around your new garden, set them only a few feet apart, so that they will immediately furnish at least a little shade and some protection from the wind. They, too, can be cut off or transplanted when they begin to crowd. This removal of surplus trees must be ruthless and thorough when the time comes. Some kinds of cut-off trees will sprout vigorously from the stump or roots, and these sprouts must be removed until the tree dies.

If there is no other way to provide shade, use a 'shade house' as described in chapter VII.

LEDGE GARDENS

If you are fortunate enough to have a shaded ledge on your property, you should certainly make a wildgarden out of it. This is especially true of granite ledges, for their slow decomposition adds acid and various plant foods to the soil and provides ideal conditions for many interesting wildflowers and ferns. However, even a limestone, marble, or other alkaline outcropping can be used to good advantage. Place over the lower parts of such a ledge a 2-inch layer of sand, cinders, or

[20]

crushed granite to carry off alkaline seepage water, and cover the drainage material with deep humus-rich acid soil to make that area suitable for acid-loving woods plants. Reserve the small caves, crevices, and shelves higher on the ledge for the not inconsiderable number of extremely interesting plants that flourish best in a neutral or slightly alkaline habitat.

Most shaded ledges, whether of granite or of one of the alkaline rocks, have certain characteristics in common. Cracks, basins, caves, and shelves abound, and the soil and surface of the northern exposure of the rock are soaking wet except in the driest part of the late summer and early fall. Nonetheless, there is good drainage and no stagnant water. Usually the soil in the crevices, shelves, and basins is shallow and consists of a bottom layer of finely granulated rock with a surface soil of almost pure humus. This combination is ideal for rock-loving plants.

V   *Collecting Wildflowers*

KNOW YOUR WILD PLANTS

The very first step in collecting any kind of woods plant is to learn its cultural requirements—the kind of soil, degree of shade, amount of moisture, temperature, acidity, and other conditions under which it will grow most luxuriantly in your garden. These conditions are given, for most worth-while cultivatable northern woods wildflowers and ferns, in Part 11 of this book.

WHERE TO GET YOUR PLANTS

It is great fun to collect the wildflowers for your own garden, and no matter how long you have been at it, you will always be able to find interesting additions to your collection. But it is essential that you gather your wild plants in such a manner that you neither encroach on the rights of others nor lessen the supply of any of the many species that have already grown too scarce.

Many states have conservation laws prohibiting the removal of rare wildflowers, ferns, and bushes. Familiarize yourself with these laws, copies of which are readily obtainable from state conservation offices. Moreover, there is a Wildflower Preservation Society of America, with many local chapters and with national headquarters at Washington, D. C. Write to the Society for its interesting literature and the name of the chapter nearest you. Join your local garden club and through it boost the cause of wildflower conservation. Then, after your garden begins to produce surplus wild plants, set them out in woodlands and along the roadsides as suggested in chapter IX.

In spite of all the legal, ethical, and common-sense restrictions, there are many places and circumstances under which you can freely collect a large variety of plants. Ideal collecting areas are those which are soon to be drained, flooded, cleared, or otherwise destroyed for necessary purposes. In such areas you may with a clear conscience collect as many specimens as you can use of any plant, no matter how rare. Moreover, you need have no hesitancy in carrying away a generous supply of leafmold, weathered stones, attractive logs, and interesting stumps. Of course you should, even under such circumstances, secure the owner's permission.

The common kinds of plants—i.e. those especially abundant in any given locality—may usually be collected in reasonable quantities without harm. For instance, false lily-of-the-valley can be safely taken from almost any patch of woodland in central New England; and Dutchmans-breeches, which are rare near most of our coastline, can be collected in reasonable quantities at many other locations. Hepaticas and spring beauties are abundant in Wisconsin.

You can supplement your collecting activities by the purchase of plants from wildflower nurseries, which obtain at least a major portion of their stock either by propagation or from areas about to be flooded or otherwise denuded of their native plants. But although nurserymen will ship your plants by parcel post or express, it is much better for you to visit the nursery yourself and have the plants lifted and protected in the manner described later in this chapter. Otherwise, the roots are likely to be stripped of earth and more or less injured, and the plants consequently set back for at least a year.

Your collection can be greatly expanded, too, through propagation by means of seeds, root cuttings, slips, and divisions—as outlined in chapter VIII. Such cuttings may be taken even from rare plants in restricted areas.

Still another good way to increase your stock of woods plants is by swapping with other gardeners. Fortunately, some plants flourish better in certain localities than in others, so that a considerable variety of plants can be exchanged in this manner with mutual profit.

WHAT TO COLLECT

Usually only plants native to your state or area should be allowed in your garden. Above all, never mix with your native plants species introduced from outside North America.

If you have a sincere interest in growing wildflowers and ferns, you can successfully cultivate any of the 200-odd species

[23]

whose appearance, habitats, and cultural requirements are described in Part ii. However, you will be well advised to direct your efforts principally toward the more easily grown species for the first year or so. But in spite of this advice to 'go slow' at first, don't hesitate to acquire any interesting plant you may espy—provided, of course, that the circumstances are such that it can be taken legitimately and without slighting either the rights of other nature lovers or the tenets of sound conservation.

WHEN TO COLLECT

Wildflowers may, with sufficient care, be transplanted at any time of the year, even when the ground is hard frozen. Generally speaking, however, it is best to collect them during their dormant seasons—that is, when they are not actively growing. Dormancy comes at different times for various kinds of plants.

Coniferous trees can best be moved immediately after their new foliage has matured—usually from the end of August to about the end of September. This permits ample time for the formation of new rootlets before freezing weather sets in.

Most deciduous trees should be transplanted during the latter part of September or early October, when their leaves are beginning to change color. However, in excessively cold areas they may best be handled in the very early spring before their buds have begun to swell. Bushes are best moved after leaf fall, when they are fully dormant.

Ferns can be transplanted at any season and wildflowers moved even when in bloom. However, the job is easier for an amateur after the plants have passed their period of active growth. Usually, early-blooming plants have become more or less dormant by the end of July. Plants like the ladyslippers, which bloom in the latter part of May or in June, cease active above-ground growth by about the first of September. Most other plants having bulbs, fleshy tubers, or long underground stems are likewise easiest to move in the late summer and early fall, preferably after their leaves have begun to sear. Very late-blooming plants, like goldenrods and asters, should be transplanted just before frost or in the spring. It is even possible, with an old ax and lots of elbow grease, to transplant woods treasures in midwinter.

[24]

COLLECTING EQUIPMENT

Although you can collect most kinds of wildflowers without any more equipment than a stout stick and your hands, a certain amount of paraphernalia will save you a lot of time and sore fingers and enable you to do a practically perfect job. Incidentally, the following suggestions presuppose that you will do your collecting from an automobile, in which there will be room for both your gear and plants. Therefore, we suggest that you always have along the following equipment and supplies.

Most important of all, you will need a long, strong, sharp trowel—sharp, to cut through hard ground and small roots, and strong so you can use some brute force in prying plants from among rocks. A narrow-bladed shovel, such as those used by nurserymen, will be a big help. Pruning shears are useful in cutting the innumerable roots that penetrate forest leafmold in every direction and which must be carefully severed if the roots of your new plant are not to be disturbed. A keen-bladed pocket knife will come in handy, especially for cutting the stakes with which you should protect the long blossom stalks of certain plants and the large fronds of some kinds of ferns.

In addition to these tools you will want one or more baskets, with stout handles, in which to carry your plants out of the woods; several wooden 'flats' or boxes in which to store them in your car; a gallon jug of water to be used in moistening roots dug from dry ground; a copy of *Growing Woodland Plants;* your soil-testing equipment; and a note book in which to jot down the exact nature of the soil in which your find was growing, the kind of vegetation with which it was most closely associated, and the depth to which it was buried.

Of every great importance, too, is a plentiful supply of bags and wrapping material, for on them will depend your ability to carry out your collecting operations successfully. First, you will need an assortment of bags of various sizes, made of watertight transparent material, such as cellophane or heavy pliofilm. Such bags can usually be purchased at food stores or at a frozen-food locker-plant, or can be made up at home. Ice-cream cartons may sometimes be conveniently used instead of small bags. For wrapping the earth balls of plants too large to go

[25]

in bags, you will want some burlap or strong old cloths and a few safety pins. Some absorbent material, such as sphagnum moss, peat, or newspapers, will also come in handy; and a couple of large burlap or cloth bags will enable you to bring home some extra woods leafmold. Large bags made of discarded plastic shower curtains are also very useful.

How to Collect

Having arrived at your chosen collecting ground with the necessary gear in your car, you may proceed as follows—assuming, for the sake of explicitness, that your first acquisition will be a pink ladyslipper. First, clear away groundlitter that might obstruct your operations. Then make a circular cut, 12 to 18 inches in diameter and about 8 inches deep, around the plant—the diameter of the cut depending on the size of the plant, and its depth on the nature of the soil where the plant is growing. There will probably be several extraneous small roots and stems to be severed by your sharp trowel; and, perhaps, one or two larger roots that must be amputated with the pruning shears.

After completing the cut around the plant, pry out the root ball, inserting your trowel first on one side and then on another. Place the plant carefully in one of your moisture-tight bags, if it is not too large. Otherwise, wrap the roots and earth in cloth or water-resistant plastic film.

Remember that no two patches of soil are exactly alike, and that your new plant will be most at home in your garden if it is surrounded there by some of the earth from which you took it. Therefore, bag a couple of quarts of the surrounding loam, number the plant and the extra soil for identification, and proceed to your next job.

Perhaps you will want to lift next a plant of partridgeberry or some other species having long underground stems. In this case do not attempt to secure a compact root ball, but instead carefully excavate the creeping stems, making certain that their sparse roots are carefully eased out of the ground, coiled without damage, and gently bagged. They must not be allowed to become dry.

Smaller wildflowers such as shinleaf, hepaticas, or rue anemone should be treated in exactly the same way as the ladyslipper. Some of these little plants have disproportionately deep roots, which must be lifted without injury.

Relatively small ferns are dug up and bagged in the same way as wildflowers of similar size. Very large ferns, like the Goldie, should have their foliage gathered together around a light stake stuck into the ground as near to the plant as possible. Then, with the foliage tied around or to the stake, the plant and stake can be lifted together and transported with a minimum of damage. Wildflowers with tall flower stalks—for example, woodlilies—can be protected in the same manner.

Creeping ferns and shrubs may be collected in the manner already suggested for partridgeberries.

There will probably be many times when you want to move seedling or young trees from the woods to your garden and you will find that many of them have long tap roots going down so far you cannot hope to outdig them. In such cases just do the best you can, and you'll be surprised how easily and quickly the plants take hold in their new surroundings. But never let the roots of small trees, especially conifers, become dry while you are moving them.

When you have got back to the car, wet the roots of all your plants thoroughly before you put them away. If the plants are in bloom, it is wise to put into the bag with them some wet absorbent material and then to close the bag up fairly tightly.

Sooner or later you are pretty sure to want to take up a plant in the dead of winter when the ground is hard frozen. That takes patience and elbow grease and is hard on your stick-to-itiveness; but it is not otherwise difficult. Just chip away the frozen earth a little at a time and slip the frozen ball into your garden in a hole previously dug and temporarily filled with leaves or other mulch.

SETTING PLANTS INTO THE GARDEN

After you are back home, promptly put your prizes in a shady spot and water them generously. Then take plenty of time to figure out the very best spot for each and every plant. Remember the gradeners' axiom: 'the right plant in the right place under the right conditions.'

When you are ready to set in the first plant, lay aside the groundlitter and dig an oversized hole, placing the excavated earth temporarily in a container for the sake of neatness. Be sure to use the stepping-stones and not to set foot on the ground.

Before setting a new plant in its hole, place under it a little of the woods soil collected with it. Then set the plant at the depth at which it was growing when found. Do not bury it too deeply. Next pack in additional soil—preferably that brought from the woods—to fill the hole, making certain that no air pockets are left around the roots.

After the plant is in place, spread groundlitter around it and water it thoroughly. If you have done a good job, the plant will be entirely at home, and there will be no indication that it has been recently transplanted.

Trailing plants and those with long underground stems require special consideration. Sometimes these trailing stems are much too long to fit into the allotted space. In that case, they may be cut into convenient lengths, each having at least one bud and some roots, or coiled into a circle of appropriate diameter. Then set the cut or coiled plant into the ground at the proper level, making sure that buds are all pointing upwards. Add the necessary depth of leafmold or woodsgarden compost. Cover the spot with groundlitter, water it plentifully, and leave the plant to redirect its growth as it sees fit.

Sometimes plants are collected as cohesive sheets of matted roots mixed with very little soil. That is frequently the case with such species as clintonia and polypody. To set these plant sheets into the garden, excavate the soil to an appropriate depth and smooth it carefully. Then lay the sheet directly on the soil and press it down gently. Sift leafmold lightly on top of the plants and drive it down toward the roots with a fairly strenuous spray of water. Work groundlitter in among the stems—and from that time on the plants should thrive as if they had never been disturbed.

VI   *Care of Woodsgardens*

Many people have the erroneous idea that because woods plants get along nicely in their native settings without any help from man they can be equally unattended in a wildflower garden. That, however, is not at all true; for in a garden these wild plants meet unaccustomed conditions, diseases, and pests with which they have not become used to coping. Therefore, wildflower gardeners must be constantly alert to provide proper shade, soil, and moisture conditions and protection against both pests and disease.

Frequent and adequate watering is the woodsgardner's all-important job. Plants just can't consume solid food. Every bit of nourishment that vegetation takes from the soil must first be dissolved in the soil water. Almost unbelievable amounts of water pass into the roots and out of the leaves of even small plants. Nearly two barrels of water are sucked from the soil to produce just one pound of clover hay. Much water, too, is required by the invisible flora of the soil—the bacteria, molds, and fungi—which must have constant dampness to function at top speed in creating humus, taking nitrogen from the air, producing foods by means of complicated chemical processes, and making those foods available to the 'higher' plants. Great quantities of water, also, must be evaporated from the groundlitter to provide the necessary coolness and high humidity at and near the surface of the ground.

Therefore wildflower gardens not only should be occasionally watered heavily to dampen the deeper soil layers, but should be sprinkled lightly several evenings a week during dry periods to permit the vegetation to freshen up during the night. Additional watering is needed in areas where tree roots are plentiful in the upper soil layers; for trees are heavy drinkers and may rob your wildflowers of their water. Moreover, the drooping branches of spruces and firs shed water so efficiently that little rain can reach the ground directly under them.

[30]

Overwatering is not much of a danger in a well-drained garden; and, on the whole, it is better to err on the side of generosity.

Not all parts of the wildgarden should receive the same amount of watering. Some plants, like the pink ladyslipper and trailing arbutus, do very well in relatively dry soil; while others, such as the beadlily and showy ladyslipper, should have their roots constantly wet. Planted crevices, shelves, and pockets in ledges should be watered generously and frequently, for under natural conditions such areas are soaked with seepage water except in the driest periods.

In view of these facts, it is obvious that there should be convenient facilities for watering your garden. This is usually no problem where only small areas are concerned. But if the gardens are fairly extensive it is desirable to lay galvanized piping or flexible hose along the paths, a few inches under the surface, and to furnish inconspicuous hose attachments at frequent intervals. Be sure that underground pipes are so arranged that they can be easily drained in the fall to keep them from freezing and bursting.

ACID CONTROL

As has been said before, correct soil reaction (acidity or alkalinity) throughout the garden is the very essence of successful cultivation of woods plants. In nature, acid content of the soil around each plant remains relatively constant over long periods; but in gardens many factors tend to change it. Therefore, it is wise frequently to test soil samples from various parts of the garden and then to take the necessary corrective steps. This is especially desirable where individual plants are not thriving as they should.

Several factors tend to lessen the acid content of garden soil. Among these are the neutralizing effects of alkaline substances dissolved in water flowing into the garden from limestone ledges, passing upward into it from non-acid subsoils, or contained in tapwater; and the action of earthworms and other animals in intermingling with the acid garden soil neutral or alkaline materials underlying it. On the other hand, the acidity of parts of the garden may increase gradually to the point where the pH is too low for such plants as yellow

[31]

ladyslipper and sharplobe hepatica. This usually comes about by the gradual removal of alkaline substances, or by the accumulation and decomposition of strongly acid needlemold or leafmold.

Fortunately, there are available several inexpensive and readily obtainable substances for altering soil acidity quickly but temporarily. Other equally convenient materials accomplish the same results very slowly but quite permanently.

Let us suppose, for instance, that after your garden has been occupied for several years by a group of plants requiring different degrees of acidity, tests indicate that the soil around the pink ladyslippers is only moderately acid (pH 5-6), while that in which yellow ladyslippers are growing has become very acid (pH 4-5). Conditions will have to be reversed quickly to save both species, for the pink 'slippers must have very acid soil, and the yellows can thrive only under slightly acid conditions, of about pH 6-7.

Corrective methods are simple. To increase the acidity (lower the pH number) of the soil around the pink ladyslippers, water them thoroughly with a solution of ½ cup of commercial superphosphate in 1 gallon of water. This solution will have an acid value of about pH 3.5 and will simultaneously increase the soil acidity (lower the pH) and give the plant a stimulating dose of phosphorus. A week later lay aside the groundlitter around the plant, dust about a level tablespoonful of equal parts of powdered sulfur and ammonium sulphate on the ground over the roots (not on the plant), and replace the groundlitter. These last-mentioned substances will maintain high acidity (low pH) for a long time. A tin can, with nail holes punched in the bottom, makes a good sifter. But remember that overdoses of aluminum, ammonium sulphate, or sulfur can injure or kill small plants.

To decrease the acidity (raise the pH number) around the yellow ladyslippers, water them a couple of times with a strong solution of ordinary garden lime, which is strongly alkaline—½ cupful to 1 gallon of water. Then sprinkle 1 heaping tablespoonful of garden lime around the plant, under the groundlitter.

The best slow-acting materials for decreasing soil acidity (raising pH) are ground limestone and ground bone. Good delayed-action acidification may be obtained by a mulch of hemlock, fir, spruce, or pine needlemold (usually about pH 4.0) applied to a depth of ¼ inch in the early spring, midsummer, and late fall.

Plant Foods

The deep, humus-rich soil of your woodsgarden will usually furnish an ample supply of the three major kinds of plant food (nitrogen, phosphorous, and potassium) and of the many minor ones. Therefore it is unnecessary to apply standard ' complete' chemical fertilizers. However, a ¼-inch mulch of pulverized cow, sheep, rabbit, chicken, or horse manure may be applied in midsummer; but, before using any animal manure around acid-loving plants, add to it about 2 heaping tablespoonfuls of powdered sulfur per bucket of manure.

Diseases and Pests

Wildflowers and ferns have not had bred into them any immunity to the diseases that attack them when brought out of the woods into close proximity with cultivated plants. Therefore, they must be guarded against disease. Various forms of fungus blight are most to be feared. Preventives and remedies are the same as those used for ordinary plants, and can be purchased from any good garden-supply store. Powdered sulfur sprinkled on the young vegetation of plants subject to fungus blight is always helpful—but unsightly.

Many sorts of pests attack cultivated wildflowers. Slugs and snails, leaf-miners, aphids, ants, rabbits, porcupines, muskrats, squirrels, rats, mice, moles, and even deer all must, under certain circumstances, be guarded against.

Slugs, snails, and cutworms spend the daylight hours hiding under the groundlitter and in the topsoil of your garden, emerging at night to nip off young shoots and to eat leaves and flowers. Ordinary insecticides, applied to the plants themselves, are not sufficiently effective against these pests. But poisoned cereal products, placed on the ground near the plants, give satisfactory control. They should be applied, strictly in accordance with manufacturer's directions, very early in the spring and at three-week intervals thereafter till wintercover is applied.

[33]

Insects are of many kinds and no one poison will control all of them. A general-purpose spray, however, will be very helpful; and your garden-supply store will recommend supplementary poisons for the hard-to-kill bugs.

Here in Gloucester we have found it wise to fence our gardens with 24-inch chicken wire each fall to keep out rabbits, removing the wire in the spring for appearance's sake. Ordinary snap traps of proper size should be used in the fall to rid the garden of rats and various kinds of small mice. Baits poisoned with red squill are also effective. Shrews are more beneficial than otherwise, for they live largely on insects, grubs, and worms, many of which are undesirable. However, don't be worried if your mouse traps catch a fairly large proportion of shrews; plenty will remain. Moles are a nuisance and should be trapped if they invade the garden.

Dogs and cats can be very troublesome. Both can be trained to stay out of your garden; and under certain circumstances the use of commercial repellents may be helpful.

Most kinds of domestic weeds find conditions in woods-gardens unfavorable, because the soil is too acid and the groundlitter too thick for them. But certain acid-loving weeds, such as sourgrass and chickweed, may become a good deal of a nuisance and must be removed promptly if they are to be kept under control. Moreover, even some wildflowers which you have yourself introduced, and which you desire to retain in reasonable quantities, may find conditions especially favorable and make great nuisances of themselves. Wild sarsaparilla-root and the bracken fern are two such plants. To prevent these rank-growers from taking over too much of your garden, it is necessary only to pull them up ruthlessly when they get out of bounds, or to enclose them by means of 9-inch galvanized-iron bands set level with the underside of the groundlitter, though the rootstocks of bracken are said sometimes to burrow a dozen feet to escape confinement!

Fire is a serious menace, for it will spread rapidly in dry groundlitter. Take every precaution against it. Watch your cigarette-smoking garden guests!

WINTERIZING

Each fall the floor of every forest and patch of woodland

is covered with a fresh layer of leaves or needles or a combination of both; and this natural mulch plays a most important part in forest life. Among other things, the deep coating of debris protects the soil from too-sudden temperature changes, and the following summer it decomposes to provide additional humus. Therefore, if your woodsflower garden is to flourish, it too should be given its fall coating of needles and leaves. Oak and beech leaves and hemlock and pine needles are best. Maple, willow, poplar, elm, and miscellaneous leaves should be used only sparingly, because they mat down tightly before spring arrives and when decomposed are only very slightly acid. The needles should be used in a layer ½ inch thick over only the more acid parts of the garden, and even there should be supplemented by a cover of about 1 inch of oak or beech leaves. As a rule, the total depth of wintercover should be from 1 to 2 inches, some or all of which should be left in place in the spring to rot. Most plants will force their way upward through such a layer but might be hampered or even smothered by thicker cover. Specific instructions regarding wintercover are given in Part 11 for most species of plants.

In many locations it will be necessary to protect the wintercover from heavy winds which would otherwise scatter the leaves far and wide. In such cases, the leaves may be held in place by a generous scattering of light twigs or branches. We have found that birch twigs are ideal and may usually be saved for use a second winter. Spruce, fir, cedar, or yew branches may also be used, but may be heavy enough, with their adherent needles, to compact the leaves unduly. All branches should be removed before spring shoots appear. Otherwise, young plants growing upward among the branches will make their removal difficult.

It is frequently desirable to protect ledge gardens, or at least parts of them, from winter winds. The method above may be used; or the leaves may be omitted and evergreen branches placed directly over the plants.

Overturned berry baskets, stained green, make excellent protection for small, isolated plants.

In windy locations, especially near the seashore, it is usually wise to protect azaleas, rhododendrons, and laurels from the full force of the wind. One excellent way is to surround the

[35]

individual plants, at least on the windiest side, with burlap windbreaks of an appropriate height. Wooden stakes can be driven into the ground before it freezes and the burlap held to the stakes by means of string or copper wire.

PLANT LABELS

As a general rule, plant labels should not be used in a woodsgarden, for they completely destroy the illusion of wildness. However, markers are needed to indicate the location of early-blooming plants whose foliage dies down during the late summer; and should also be set out in the fall to indicate unoccupied garden areas that may be planted early the following spring.

When markers are used, they should be both inconspicuous and rot-resistant. Standard flat markers about 6 inches long will be satisfactory if their lower ends are dipped in tree paint. Cedar or cypress stakes stained brown will last almost indefinitely; or you can make very satisfactory markers out of ½-inch-thick oak twigs whittled flat on one side and pointed at the lower end. Remove markers during seasons they are not needed.

PICKING FLOWERS

Very few wildflower gardeners will want to cut the blossoms from either their own plants or those they find in the woods. However, many kinds of woodsflowers can be picked without damage to the plant, provided that none of the leaves are cut and the roots are not disturbed. Never try to pull or break off the blossoms—use a sharp knife or scissors.

Shade-Houses

A 'shade-' or 'lath-' house is an artificial shelter for plants requiring shade and protection from wind. These houses are essentially brush- or lath-roofed arbors, usually enclosed on two or three sides to provide shade of controllable density. Under the houses are located plant beds of varying soil characteristics.

Shade-houses are very convenient accessories in the cultivation of woodland plants and a necessity in commercial wild-flower propagation. In fact, they are so convenient and conditions under them can be controlled so accurately that some amateurs use them extensively.

Although shade-houses may vary greatly in size, shape, material, and construction, the average amateur gardener will find that a house built as follows is inexpensive, easy to construct, and of many uses. It is a sloping-roofed, three-sided

Shade-House Frame

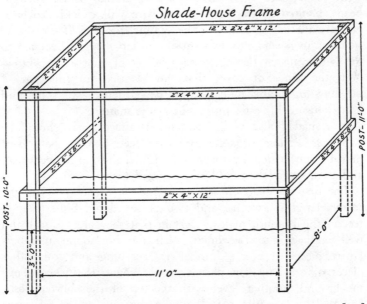

shed, the highest side being open and facing north. Ground dimensions are 8 x 11 feet; the open side is 11 feet long and 8 feet high; and the low side is 7 feet high. The corner posts are of cedar or locust sunk 3 feet in the ground. Horizontal members are 2 x 4 beams painted brown. The roof and sides may be of trimmed sapling poles—cedar or gray birch will do very nicely—placed sufficiently close together to give just the right amount of shade on each of the shade-house beds. The roof saplings may be merely laid in place on the frame, but those on the side should be wired or nailed loosely to the frame so that they can be easily moved as changed shade conditions are required. Laths, matting, brush, burlap, plastic seran netting, growing vines, or other convenient material may be used instead of poles. Because shade is required principally during the summer months, the ends and south side of the house may be left more or less open during winter and spring and densely shaded during the summer by annual vines planted against them. One good method of accomplishing this is to make the ends and south side of saplings spaced several inches apart and covered with chicken wire on the outside. During the winter, the poles themselves will furnish sufficient light shade; and early in the spring annual vines, such as beans, planted at the base of the wire will quickly cover it and provide dense shade for the summer months. If the shade-house is in a very windy location, burlap may be fastened to the wire walls of the house to a height of 3 or 4 feet. However, the kinds of cover that can be used for this sort of building are many indeed, and the gardener will soon find himself using his own judgment in the matter.

In a shade-house of the dimensions above, there should be two beds, each approximately 5 x 8 feet. One or both beds may be subdivided by means of metal bands into two areas, and a sunken path should run between them.

The first construction step is to cut the corner posts to the correct lengths—two 10 and two 11 feet long. Sink them 3 feet in the ground, making certain that they are vertical and well tamped into the holes. Nail the horizontal members (three pieces of 2 x 4 lumber 12 feet long and four other pieces 9 feet long) in place, one set about 18 inches above the ground, another level with the top of the shorter posts, and the third 12-foot piece between the tops of the tall posts to form a rest for the high side of the roof. Of course, no 2 x 4 piece is placed near the ground on the northern side of the house, which is to remain open and unobstructed.

Next, excavate the soil from the floor of the house to a depth of about 8 inches. Make the side walls of the excavation as vertical as possible, and against them all around the excavation and around the posts place an 8-inch-wide strip of galvanized iron (coated with tree paint, especially on the cut edges) and peg it snugly against the walls. Tree roots and large boulders must be removed from the excavation.

Now place a 2 x 8 inch plank 8 feet long on each side of a foot-wide path running across the middle of the excavation from front to back. Peg the planks in place. This will form two beds, each 5½ x 8 feet with a path between them.

Next, screen the excavated dirt through ½-inch mesh to remove roots, stones, and other debris. Put back into the excavation a 2-inch layer of the coarse material, to aid drainage. Add cinders, sand, or crushed granite if necessary to complete the 2-inch layer. Then build up a soil mixture totaling 16 inches in depth, as directed on pp. 13–14.

When the beds have been completed, spread a 2-inch layer of crushed stone (about ½ inch mesh), sand, or cinders on the path and cover it with 2 inches of pine needles or leaves. Add 8-inch-wide planks all around both beds, which should have been built up about that much above the surrounding ground, level off the soil in the beds, put a few stepping-stones in place, and let the soil settle for at least two weeks.

Then, as instructed elsewhere, determine the acidity of the soil, which will probably be moderately acid, testing between pH 5 and 6. Adjust one bed to about pH 4.5 for plants requiring very acid conditions. Divide the second bed into two parts by means of a metal strip and bring one part to pH 5.5 and the other to pH 6.5. This may be done by adding about 2 cupfuls per square yard of an equal mixture of powdered sulfur and ammonium sulphate to lower the pH about 1 point, or 3 cupfuls of garden lime to raise the pH 1 point. Some experimentation will be required to bring about just the desired degree of acidity in each bed.

Finally, add groundlitter and stepping-stones to the beds, and they will be ready for use.

VIII   *Propagation*

Generally speaking, wildflowers are propagated by the same
methods used for domesticated plants—i.e. seeds, root and
stem cuttings, division, and layering. More often than not,
annuals and biennials are grown from seed, while perennials
are more commonly increased by one or more of the other
methods. For your guidance, the text of Part II suggests the
preferred methods of propagating each species of plant described therein.

PROPAGATING FROM SEEDS

Seeds, like unborn infants, are living embryos. Leaf, stem, and
root are all present in even the tiniest seed, ready to start active
growth the moment conditions are propitious. Food sufficient
to nourish the young plant until its roots and leaves begin
to function is present in an unbelievably concentrated form;
and both embryo and food are contained in a shell or coating
admirably adapted to carry the young plant through adversi-
ties that would surely prove fatal were such protection lacking.

Some seeds—like those of the orange or maple—will die
unless permitted to germinate very soon after ripening. Others
are extremely long-lived. Wild morning-glory seeds, buried for
30 years by the U.S. Department of Agriculture, sprouted two
days after being 'exhumed'; and lotus seeds have produced
vigorous plants after lying deep in a bog for an estimated 400
years.

Many seeds have extraordinarily resistant shells. Chokecher-
ries and hundreds of other species of plants are spread by seeds
eaten by birds and later evacuated some distance away; and
one kind of large tropical seed may survive several months'
submersion in the ocean.

Some seeds are extremely minute and incredibly numerous.
A single ladyslipper blossom, for instance, produces such
myriads of dust-fine seeds that if all were to germinate and
mature, they would, within a couple of generations, carpet

[40]

every available square foot of woodland. Other seeds, however, are of relatively tremendous size and produced in only small numbers—as witness the coconut.

Many seeds are ripe when they fall to the ground, but others normally require several years to complete their development. Some kinds are killed by even moderately low temperatures, while others regularly survive our coldest northern winters, and may even require prolonged exposure to low temperatures before germination can occur.

Thus it is evident that no brief discussion of propagation by means of seeds can be more than suggestive. But each seed-bearing species has attuned its seeding habits, over scores of thousands of years, to its environment. Therefore even the most inexperienced woodsgardener can attain fair successs by noting carefully each species' natural seeding habits and combining the knowledge thus gained with the following simple instructions.

Some inexpensive equipment and supplies are needed for propagating plants from seeds, and it is wise to assemble all of that material before starting operations.

First, of course, you will have to collect your seed, presumably from plants growing in the woods. For that purpose you should have some medium-sized envelopes (e.g. 3½ x 6½ inches) with gummed flaps. Put the seeds in the envelopes as soon as collected, and keep them there till planted. Be sure that the flaps are tightly closed, so that no seeds will be lost. On each envelope write all necessary data: name of plant, date and location, condition and pH of soil immediately around the parent plant, depth and nature of groundlitter and leafmold, and any other facts you think may later prove useful.

Some stout cloth or waterproof paper bags will come in handy for collecting about a bucketful of topsoil from around each plant—or kind of plant—from which seed is taken. Bag and seed-envelope should be similarly identified, for later the seed will be planted in the soil in which its parent plants grew.

You will need some three-inch flower pots in which to plant the seeds and give the seedlings a good start. Each pot will do for from 5 to 9 seeds, depending on their size. Larger or smaller pots may of course be used if desired.

A package each of seed disinfectant such as 'Semesan' and of root hormone such as 'Rootone' will be needed, and can be purchased from any seed store.

Now let us consider the soil—natural or synthetic—in which your seeds are to be planted and grown. Such soil should be humus-rich, free from coarse materials, uncompacted, and of approximately the same reaction (pH) as that just below the groundlitter where the parent plants grew. Of course, the top-soil taken from near each of the plants from which your seed was collected would be ideal. But the chances are against your having enough such 'natural' soil available, so you will need the ingredients from which to prepare a synthetic product.

First, you must have a goodly quantity—several quarts at least—of clean, sharp builders' sand. It will be used as a drainage layer in the lower part of each pot or box, and for other purposes. Then you must have a supply of one of the following—named in the order of their desirability: woodsgarden compost (see chapter 11); natural leafmold; or granulated peat.

An assortment of miscellaneous materials will include: bits of broken pots or crockery, or small stones, to prevent loss of sand through the drainage holes in pot-bottoms; cellophane to cover pots after the seeds are planted; your pH-testing kit to determine soil reaction (pH); a little lime to raise the pH, if necessary, and some ammonium sulphate to lower it; and a small sieve—just a 12 x 12 inch piece of ¼-inch-mesh woven wire, which can be bought at any hardware store—through which to strain the sand and soil.

All containers and materials used in seed planting must be sterilized, to protect disease-sensitive seedlings. This is accomplished by oven-baking the pots, sand, bits of broken pottery, and small stones for one hour at 300°, and the soil ingredients for two hours at about 225°–250°. Sterilization of soil-filled pots may be conveniently accomplished by steaming for 30 minutes in a pressure canner.

Now, having assembled some seeds and all the needed supplies, materials, and accessories, you are almost ready to start actual planting operations. But first a word or two about *when* to plant.

From the time-to-plant point of view, all woods-wildflower seeds may be separated into two groups—those of the early-blooming species and those that do not ripen till late summer or fall. The former may usually be planted as soon as gathered, and will form fair-sized seedlings by fall. Most of the latter require a long dormant period at low temperature, and should therefore be planted when collected and left outdoors over winter—about which more later.

Now you are ready to fill the pots. Partly plug the bottom holes with a piece of broken pottery or a small stone, to prevent loss of soil while permitting ample drainage. Add a ¼-inch layer of unsifted granulated peat or leafmold, and, over that, ¾ inches of sand. Then fill the pot levelful with one of the following: (a) sifted soil from around the plants from which the seed was taken; (b) a mixture of 3 parts sifted woods-garden compost and 1 part sand; or (c) equal parts of sand and sifted peat or shredded sphagnum moss. Tap the pot gently to settle its contents and further press down the soil till it is about ¾ inches below the top.

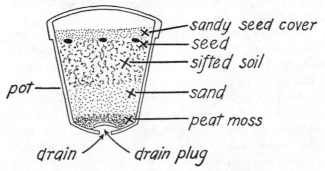

At this stage of the proceedings the pot and its contents will probably be bone-dry as the result of sterilization. So set one or more pots in a biscuit pan and add about ½ inch of water, which will quickly be absorbed by the sand and soil. Add more water if and when necessary, till the pot and its contents are damp (but not soaking wet) to the top. Then drain to remove any excess moisture.

It is during the soaking operation that the acidity of the soil in the pot can be adjusted to the desired point by acidifying the water to pH 4–5 with ammonium sulphate if you wish to make the soil more acid, or by adding a little lime if you want to make the pot contents less acid (raise the pH).

Now dust the seed with disinfectant and root hormone, by placing a pinch of each in the envelope and shaking the seed around in it.

Place one seed on the surface of the soil in the center of each pot, and from 4 to 8 around it, depending on the seed size. Then sift (using a coarse kitchen strainer) equal parts of sand and woods-compost (or woods soil or granulated peat) evenly over the seeds to a depth equal to about 4 times the diameter of the seed. Never plant more than one kind of seed in a single pot.

Now over each pot fasten a piece of cellophane and poke one or more holes through it with a pencil—to conserve moisture while permitting 'breathing.' Rubber bands are a convenient means of fastening covers to the pots. Set the pots (still in pans) in a shady spot, indoors or out, and await results. Never let the soil either dry out or become soggy. Just the right amount of water—always placed in the pan and never directly in the pots—is essential to successful germination.

The pot-filling and seed-planting procedure as described above applies equally to the seeds of both spring- and fall-blooming plants. But in the case of the fall bloomers the cellophane-covered pots should be buried to their tops in a wind-free shady spot of ground out of doors. Then, before the first hard freeze, a square of ¼-inch mesh wire should be laid across the tops of the pots and 6 or 8 inches of oak or beech leaves piled on the wire and held in place with evergreen boughs, or some equally effective means. This arrangement will closely simulate nature's process for carrying fall-ripened seeds over the winter by exposing them to low temperatures, keeping them constantly moist, and protecting them from the 'heaving' action of soil that is repeatedly frozen and thawed.

Just as soon, in the spring, as danger of severe frost has passed, the leaf cover should be removed gradually and the seeds left to sprout—still with each pot covered with cellophane.

After the seeds have sprouted, remove the cellophane, but do not disturb the seeds until the fourth leaf has appeared. Then transplant each seedling into a separate pot, filled with a mixture of 2 parts of oak or beech leafmold or woodsgarden compost, 1 part sand, and 1 part garden soil. No sand should be placed in the pot-bottom, and the soil should not be sterilized. Acidity may be brought to the proper point for the species (see Part II) by watering once or twice with a pH 3.5 solution of ammonium sulphate or a weak lime-water solution as explained above. Thereafter the potted plants may be set in the woodsgarden or in any other appropriately shaded outdoors location, and watered regularly. By about 15 September they should be removed from their pots and placed in permanent locations. Of course they may be unpotted sooner if there has been sufficient growth.

Propagating by Division

In horticultural language 'division' refers to the method of increasing plants by subdividing large clusters into several individuals. It is probably the most common method of increasing wildflowers and ferns.

Division is carried out most easily and advantageously while plants are dormant, or at least while their aboveground portions are not growing actively. Making divisions is very simple—the clumps are merely pulled apart, or separated by severing the rootstock in appropriate places.

After plants have been divided, they may be reset in the garden or in pots and, if the job has been carefully done, should continue their growth with little interruption.

Propagating by Cuttings

This is a method of increasing plants by causing sections of the stem to root and generate new individuals having inheritance characteristics substantially identical with the plants from which the cuttings are taken. Many types of trees, shrubs, herbs, and ferns can be readily and very rapidly multiplied by cuttings of one kind or another.

Several types of cuttings are in frequent use. Softwood cuttings are those taken from the ends of actively growing stems. Hardwood cuttings are similar, but are made in the fall of the year from matured stems. Root cuttings are segments of underground stems or rootstocks. The following suggestions are applicable to all kinds.

Cuttings may be started in pots, shallow wooden boxes

[45]

called 'flats,' or an outdoor bed. Soil should be composed of two parts of sand and one part woodsgarden compost, beech or oak leafmold, or granulated peat. The resulting mixture should be oven-sterilized in a shallow pan for two hours at about 225°–250°, and should then be dampened and brought to the appropriate pH for each species of plant (see Part II) by the use of acidulated or alkalized water as previously suggested under 'Propagating from Seeds.'

All kinds of cuttings should be treated, before planting, with a mixture of root-producing hormone and a disinfectant. Both are available at seed stores, and the manufacturers' directions must be followed exactly. After planting, cuttings must be kept constantly damp but not soaking wet. Keep the air around them humid by covering them with cellophane caps, or glass jars or tumblers. An aquarium, topped by cellophane pierced by several pencil holes, makes an excellent propagating case for cuttings. Moderate shade is necessary, but the cuttings should never be kept in the dark and should be given some sunlight after the first new leaves appear.

When cuttings have become well rooted and have begun to grow vigorously, they may be transplanted into individual containers or set directly into the woodsgarden. Thereafter they are cared for in the same way as adult plants.

With these general instructions in mind, let us now consider in some detail each of the several types of cuttings.

Softwood cuttings are the familiar 'slips' of the amateur gardener. They should be taken from the end of a growing branch, have from 4 to 6 nodes, and be from 3 to about 6 inches long—unless the nodes are so far apart that longer pieces are necessary. The lowermost leaves should be removed and the upper ones left undisturbed, or cut in half if they are very large. Stems should be cut with a sharp knife and at right angles. With most plants this type of cutting may be made at almost any time during active growth; but softwood cuttings should be taken from azaleas, rhododendrons, and certain other woody plants only when the stems are sufficiently mature to snap when bent. Two or three nodes should be buried and a similar number left above ground.

Hardwood cuttings are made in the fall from the ends or near the ends of branches of the current year's growth and are not as a rule planted directly in cutting beds. Instead, they are usually tied in bundles of from six to a dozen and placed in damp sand or a mixture of sand and humus in a cool cellar with a temperature ranging from about 35° to 50° F., or are buried outdoors below frost line in a well-drained area. During the winter months 'callousing' of the lower end of each cutting takes place—a sort of natural healing process preliminary to the formation of roots. As soon as the ground outdoors has thawed, these hardwood cuttings are removed from their winter beds, separated, and planted two or three nodes deep either in outdoor cutting beds or at appropriate spots in the garden. A glass jar placed up-side-down over each cutting will furnish welcome protection against the evaporation of life-giving stem juices.

Even hardwood cuttings sometimes do well if placed directly in the woodsgarden late in the fall; but such cuttings should be covered by an inverted glass jar, which in turn must be protected by a deep layer of oak or beech leaves so held in place that wind cannot blow them away.

It is, of course, important that cutting beds be of approximately the same degree of acidity to which the parent plants are accustomed; and hardwood cuttings, like those from softwood, should receive some protection from too-rapid moisture loss through evaporation.

Root cuttings are not made from true roots but from creeping underground stems or rootstocks, or from tubers. Each cutting is a section—terminal or otherwise—several inches long and having one or more nodes, buds, or sprouts. Somewhat

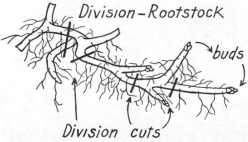

similar cuttings are made from the prone surface-creeping stems of such plants as trailing arbutus, twinflower, wild-ginger, and partridgeberry. Segments of such stems frequently are already rooted to some extent, and these roots should be carefully buried when the cutting is laid on the ground and then lightly covered with a mixture of equal parts of sand and leafmold or compost.

Root cuttings may best be taken while the plants are dormant in late summer or very early spring. Spring cuttings may bloom the same year; but those made in the summer usually do not blossom till the next season.

Cuttings of this type may be planted in outdoor beds or in flats in the same type of soil and at the depth from which they were originally taken. It is essential that such soil be humus-rich, uncompacted, and of appropriate pH. The surface of the bed or flat should never become dry; and to keep it moist nothing is better than a sheet of cellophane in which a few pencil holes have been punched. Small stones may be used to hold the covering out of actual contact with the soil.

Fall-made root cuttings should be wintered outdoors, protected with a generous leafy wintercover which is removed in the spring as soon as all danger of a freeze has passed. Active growth should commence soon thereafter.

Layerings may be described as cuttings that are rooted while still attached to, and securing nourishment from, the parent plant. Three methods of layering are commonly used. A branch may be bent to the ground and partly buried; the tip only may be buried; or the base of a plant having multiple stems may be mounded over with soil.

Before a layering is made, it is well to injure the stem

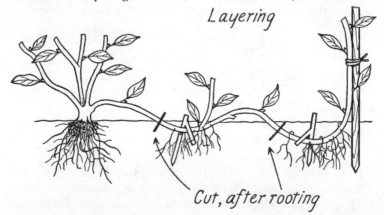

Layering

Cut, after rooting

slightly and apply Rootone to it at the points where rooting is expected. The depth to which the to-be-rooted area is buried depends on the size of the parent plant and on other factors which you will soon learn from observation and experience. For instance, a partridgeberry stem might be covered only ½ inch deep and a small piece of cellophane laid over it; but a rhododendron branch should be buried 4 to 6 inches. The soil around layerings should be kept constantly damp.

Layered creeping plants, such as partridgeberry, sometimes root within a few weeks, but woodier plants like rhododendrons may require 18 months or longer. In any event, when a good root growth has been obtained, the rooted section is severed from the parent plant and established in a nursery or in the garden itself.

Although it is easy for even a beginner, using the methods so sketchily outlined above, to multiply many kinds of wildflowers and ferns rapidly, the whole question of plant propagation is so broad that every woodsgardener should learn more about it than we have space for here. Many textbooks have been written on the subject; and two such works, by Hottes, worded and illustrated so the most inexperienced gardener can understand them—yet adequate for a professional—are listed under 'Recommended Reading.' Methods of growing ferns from spores are described under 'Ferns' in Part II.

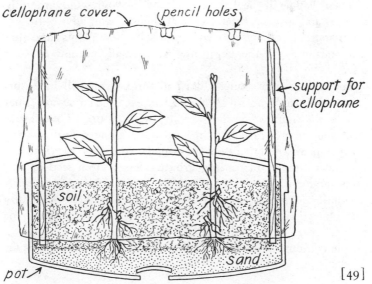

Using Surplus Plants

Many kinds of wildflowers and ferns, even some rare and delicate species that happen to find conditions in your garden unusually favorable, will multiply so rapidly that you will soon have a surplus. In the authors' garden this has been true of several species of solomonseal, wildginger, bloodroot, false lily of the valley, twinleaf, oakfern, rusty woodsia, and narrowleaf beechfern. Moreover, you will surely want to try your hand at various methods of propagation—by seeds, cuttings, layerings, and division—and even moderate success with any of these processes will quickly increase your stock.

At first you will use these homegrown plants around your own premises; there are innumerable interesting ways to do so. Divisions of the large wildflowers and ferns will fill in too-large bare spots, creepers will form an interesting and graceful groundcover, and small flowering herbs will be just right in nooks and angles along the paths and borders. Or, if your first garden was small and is already full, you will certainly feel the urge to start new ones.

Then you will begin to trade with your wildgardening friends, and give neighbors enough plants—and advice—to get them started. Perhaps you will even sell a few plants; and that tiny start may be the beginning of a small business of your own.

But at last—and sooner than you think—you will have surpluses that can't be sold, traded, or even given away. That will be the time to begin 'swapping with nature.' Then, every time you start on a collecting trip, take along a few of your surplus plants suitable for the woods you plan to visit. Do you have some extra trailing arbutus, raised from seed or cuttings; and are you going to search some mixed pine-and-oak woods for pink ladyslippers? If so, swap an arbutus—carefully transplanted into the humus-rich soil under a white pine—for each 'slipper. Or would you like to exchange a beadlily for a purple trillium? Both grow in deep, rich, oak-and-beech woods.

How about taking along some of your surplus giant solomon-seal and bringing back a clump of twinleaf?

This 'swapping with nature' is fun; and it is also sound conservation. Your woodsgarden surpluses of wildflowers and ferns, skilfully introduced in just the right wild areas, can spread rapidly and re-establish many interesting plants previously exterminated from those particular woods. Seek—and we think you will surely obtain—the co-operation of managers of parks, public reservations, wildlife refuges, state forests, and private owners of woodlands. You can thus give back to the woods many more plants than you take from them, while increasing your own collection and gaining invaluable experience.

Indoor forcing, in connection with our northern woods plants, means bringing them into bloom indoors during the winter. More often than not, wildflowers and ferns so treated are either killed or so seriously retarded that they do not resume normal growth for several years. Therefore the practice is justifiable only under special circumstances.

But many people, especially shut-ins and invalids, derive great pleasure from watching woods plants sprout, flourish, and bloom while winter howls outdoors. Even the experienced woodsgardener may like to ride his hobby while the garden is buried deep in snow.

Not all woodland plants are rare or in danger of becoming so; and many of the commoner kinds can be used for forcing without damaging the cause of sound conservation. Moreover, every successful woodsgardener will produce surplus plants that may well be used for this purpose.

Most northern woods plants require a long dormant season each fall and winter, and many must be subjected to freezing temperatures if they are to bloom normally after being brought indoors. Several years ago the authors winterforced three hepatica plants that had been growing side-by-side and were in every way comparable. One plant was brought indoors about Thanksgiving, before there had been even one hard freeze. That plant rotted without sprouting. A second was dug from lightly frozen ground in the middle of December. It sent up stunted leaves, but did not bloom. The third plant, however, chopped out with a ball of frozen earth in mid-January, rewarded us with numerous bluish-purple blossoms and a mass of normal foliage.

With this experience—and many others—in mind we suggest that you proceed as follows. About the first of October decide what plants you are going to force, how you are going to arrange and associate them, and in what pots or boxes you will put them. Then lift the plants as suggested in chapter v, and

set them in the containers in which they are later to be taken indoors. Do not disturb their roots more than absolutely necessary, and give them plenty of the same soil in which they were growing.

When the job of transplanting is finished, sink the containers in compacted oak leaves or some other suitable material in a well-drained and shaded outdoor pit or coldframe. Then thoroughly water both the containers and the surrounding material with a solution of commercial superphosphate of the same pH value as that of the soil in which the plants were growing. Mulch well with oak leaves, and leave everything 'as is' till about New Years. Meanwhile, keep the soil moist. Also, keep mice away!

There won't be too much difficulty in removing the containers from the frozen mulch. Then bring them indoors and keep them in the coolest spot available for a week or ten days. Next place them where they will have some sun—and watch 'em grow!

Almost any kind of containers may be used for indoor forcing: standard flower pots, window boxes, wooden flats, berry boxes, terrariums,* and even tin cans. Good drainage is essential; and an outer wrapping of metal foil will both give unglazed pots and wooden boxes an attractive appearance and aid in retaining moisture.

Potted plants need the same soil pH indoors as out. You made a good start in that direction when you used wildgarden loam for potting, but soil acidity must also be kept constant while the plants are in the house. Circumstances will dictate the most feasible way of accomplishing this. A little powdered sulfur sprinkled on the soil will meet the situation for plants requiring acidities of pH 4–5. Water acidified to about pH 5.5 with superphosphate will properly adjust the soil for plants that thrive under moderately acid conditions; and those that do best with little or no acid may be moistened with tapwater to which lime has been added.

The time required for woods plants to bloom after being brought indoors cannot be accurately stated here. It will depend both on the kind of plant and on the temperature and the

* See *The Garden Encyclopedia* (Wm. H. Wise & Co.) for detailed suggestions about terrariums.

amount of sunlight to which it is exposed. Generally speaking, wild flowers that normally bloom in early spring will grow rapidly indoors. Late bloomers like the solomonseals may require six weeks or more. Most ferns begin to uncoil their fiddlehead-shaped fronds in a week or two. Hepaticas may be blossoming in as little as five days.

If all of the plants used for indoor forcing are of plentiful varieties or part of your own surplus production, they may be thrown away when they have served their purpose. But if they are rare, you should make every effort to keep them alive till they can be reset outdoors. This may be difficult with the early-blooming kinds, and relatively easy with late-blossoming species and with ferns. In either case all you can do is to nurse them along till they can be returned to the garden after danger of hard frosts has passed; and, when you do set them out, be sure not to dig up some other plant in the process!

PART TWO

Descriptions, Habitats, and Cultural Requirements of Woods Wildflowers and Ferns

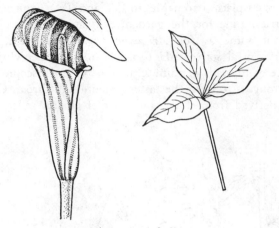

Arisaema triphyllum

Jack-in-the-Pulpit; Indian Turnip (*Arisae'ma triphyl'lum*)

This familiar wet-ground, soft-fleshed plant has 1 or 2 large leaves, each divided into 3 leaflets attached to a single stalk which rises to a height of 12 to 36 inches from a disc-shaped perennial root. Blossom is a large cylindrical, brown-striped, hooded, compound flower growing between the leaves. Blooms in May and June. Fruit a cluster of bright red berries. This and two closely related species are found in wet spots in woods, along streams, and in meadows. One species has unstriped green flowers. Range: eastern N.A.

The common names are derived respectively from the shape of the flower and the fact that Indians after slicing, drying, and cooking the very acrid tubers, used them for food.

An excellent woodsgarden plant, very easy to cultivate and requiring little care. Propagation by root division and from seed. Thrives under a variety of conditions, but prefers humus-rich soil of pH 5–6, partial shade, and plenty of moisture. Heavy, leafy wintercover, left in place.

Green Dragon (*Arisae'ma dracon'tium*)

A close relative of the jack-in-the-pulpit, this plant has a single much-divided leaf rising from a tuberous root to a height of 2–4 feet. Blossom is greenish and resembles that of the jack-in-the-pulpit, but is narrower and has a long, upward-pointing 'tongue.' Blooms June and July. Found in wet decidous woods and in open places, from Me. to Fla. and Tex. Fruit is orange-red berries. Fine for the garden, cultivation and propagation being the same as for *Arisaema triphyllum*. Rich, slightly acid, or neutral soil of pH 6–7. The root juice, owing to the presence of myriads of minute, needle-like microscopic crystals, is so strong as to burn the taster's mouth and throat. Common names derived from shape and color of bloom.

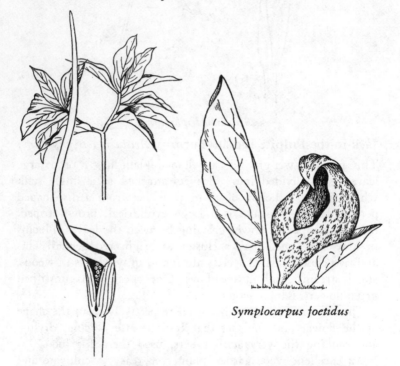

Symplocarpus foetidus

Arisaema dracontium

Skunkcabbage (*Symplocar'pus foe'tidus*)

A rank-smelling, heavy-rooted perennial with a clump of large (up to 24 inches long) broadly oval leaves, and a large mottled

[58]

purple-bronze-green hooded bloom which appears at the ground surface in early spring. Found in wet, moderately acid to neutral (pH 5–7) muck of swamps, bog margins, and open, flooded, deciduous woods. Ranges from N.S. to Ont., and south to N.C., Minn., and Iowa. Readily cultivated in a large, partly shaded, very wet area. No care required, and will readily reproduce itself by seed. The unusual bloom pokes up through mud and water even before the leaves are grown.

Tradescantia virginiana

Virginia Spiderwort; Spiderlily (*Tradescan'tia virginia'na*)

A large but dainty perennial up to 36 inches high, with long, narrow, bright-green leaves springing alternately from a slender branched stalk ascending erectly from a stout creeping rootstock and topped by a group of short-stemmed blue or purplish (rarely white) flowers up to 2 inches across. Blooms June to August. Open woods and thickets from N.Y., Ohio, and S.D. to Va. and Ark.

This is a common plant in cultivation, and does well in a semi-shaded spot with humus-rich soil of pH 6–7. Culture is easy, with propagation by root divisions, seeds, and softwood cuttings (or slips). Wintercover permissible but not necessary.

Several other native and introduced spiderworts occur in the northern U.S. Care should be exercised to keep these foreign species out of the woodsgarden. Under favorable conditions spiderworts spread so rapidly as to require control.

[59]

Woodrush (*Lu'zula campes'tris*)

An inconspicuous grass-like perennial having a basal cluster of long, hairy, narrow leaves and a sparsely leaved stalk bearing at its top a group of tiny inconspicuous greenish flowers later developing 3-seeded capsules. Prefers slightly acid soil (pH 6–7) on open wooded slopes over much of N.A., Europe, and Asia.

Easily cultivated and interesting as a groundcover. Requires no special care, and does well in most woods soils.

Turkeybeard Beargrass (*Xerophyl'lum asphodeloi'des*)

The smooth, hyacinth-like blossom stalk, topped by a dense cylindrical mass of tiny white flowers, springs, with a tight rosette of grass-like leaves, from a thick perennial, woody underground stem. Blooms in May. Height up to 5 feet. Rich, very acid soil under pines or oaks, from N.J. to Fla. and Tenn. Will grow in the woodsgarden in soil of pH 4–5.

Luzula campestris   *Xerophyllum asphodeloides*

Fairywand; Blazing Star (*Chamaeli'rium lu'teum*)

In this lily-like plant both a rosette of oval leaves and a 2 to 3 foot flower stalk, topped with a narrow spike of small white flowers, rise from a fleshy rootstock. Blooms in June. Seed pods are tiny capsules. Wet, open woods, in humus-rich soil of pH

[60]

5–6, from Mass. to Fla. and Ark. Requires relatively little care in cultivation. Benefits from an oakleaf wintercover. Propagation by division.

Chamaelirium luteum   *Amianthium muscaetoxicum*

Crowpoison; Flypoison; Poison-Lily
(*Amian'thium muscaetox'icum*)

The long, narrow leaves and 12 to 24 inch flower stalk of this member of the lily family superficially resemble those of the common hyacinth, and rise from an elongated bulb. Flowers are first white, then bronzy-green. Blooms May and June. Rich open woods in very acid soil from N.Y. to Fla. and Ark. Suitable for an acid woodsgarden, in semi-shade. Cultivation easy if soil is kept at pH 4–5. Propagated by division and, more difficultly, from seed. Common names come from old-time use of crushed bulbs as poison.

Grassleaf Stenanthium; Featherfleece
(*Stenan'thium grami'neum*)

One to several feet high, with grass-like alternate leaves on a stalk topped by a branched spike of tiny white flowers later becoming green. Blooms in July. Wet, open woods with very

[61]

acid humus-rich soil of pH 4–5. Ranges from Pa. and Ohio south. A good, relatively pest-free plant for a semi-shaded wet spot. Propagation by division.

Stenanthium gramineum   *Uvularia sessilifolia*

Little Merrybells, or Sessile-Leaved Bellwort
(*Uvula'ria sessilifo'lia*)

This delightful little plant thickly carpets moist deciduous woods and thickets having deep humus-rich, moderately acid soil. The 6 to 12 inch stalks spring from long slender rootstocks, are usually two-branched, clasped by leaf scales below and with small sessile, ovate, alternate leaves above. The pale-yellow flowers are usually single, but may be paired, and hang bell-like on short stems from leaf bases. Blossoms in early spring, and fruit is a three-sided capsule which persists till the plant is frost-killed. On Cape Ann merrybells and troutlilies are often intermingled. Range: New Brunswick and Ont. south to Ga., Minn., and Ark.

Although somewhat difficult to transplant because of its long underground stems, little merrybells should do well in a damp, shady, well-watered part of your garden. Wintercover should be of hardwood leaves, left in place the following spring.

Merrybells are so plentiful that propagation is usually not

justified. But if you wish to do so, you can multiply the plants either 'from seed, which should be planted when ripe, or from root cuttings. Apparently optimum pH 5–6.

Uvularia grandiflora   *Allium canadense*

Big Merrybells; Large-Flowered Bellwort
(*Uvula'ria grandiflo'ra*)

This species differs from the foregoing principally in being larger, reaching a height of 2 feet; in having clasping leaves whose bases ring the stalk, and which are finely hairy on their undersides; and in having larger and yellower flowers. Blooms in April and May, and is thoroughly suitable for cultivation; but should have neutral or only slightly acid soil. Range: Que. to Ont., and south to Ga., Kans., and Minn. Optimum pH 6–7.

Canada Garlic; Wild Garlic (*Al'lium canaden'se*)

In this onion the sparse cluster of grass-like leaves and the 8 to 12 inch blossom stalk grow from a small globular bulb. Blossom is a mixed cluster of lavender flowers and bulblets. Blooms in May. Open woods and fields from New Brunswick to Tex. Can be easily cultivated in at least moderately rich approximately neutral soil—pH 6.5–7.0.

[63]

Wild Leek; Wood Leek (*Al'lium tricoc'cum*)

Two narrowly oval, veined leaves appear in early spring from an elongated white bulb, and wither away before the smooth 12-inch flower stalk reaches maximum development in July. Small white flowers in a flattish terminal cluster. Rich open woods from New Brunswick to Minn., and south to N.C. and Mo. Prefers soil of pH 6–7. A good garden plant, propagated by seed and by division. Wintercover desirable. Crushed foliage and bulb have strong onion flavor and may be eaten. Plant locations should be marked before blossom stalk disappears.

Allium tricoccum   *Nothoscordum bivalve*

Yellow False Garlic; Scentless Garlic
(*Nothoscor'dum bival've*)

Very narrow, grass-like leaves, 6 to 16 inches long, and a smooth flower stalk of similar length, springing from a perennial bulbous base. Small, starry, white flowers in a flat, terminal cluster. Blooms in April and May in grasslands and open deciduous woods from Va. to Fla. and Mex. A good woods-garden plant, hardy in northern states if given leafy wintercover. Juice odorless and tasteless. Rich soil of pH 6–7.

[64]

Wood Lily; Orangecup Lily (*Lil'ium philadel'phicum*)

This is a true lily, found in humus-rich, very acid, well-drained soil in dry open woods and clearings. Its stalk rises from a scaly bulb to a height of 2 to 3 feet, and is topped by from 1 to 4 upright, cup-shaped, spotted orange-red flowers. Leaves are long and narrow, in whorls on the stalk. A related midwestern species is closely similar but has scattered, rather than whorled, leaves. Fruit a pod. Blooms July to Aug. Range: Me., Ont., and B.C. south to N.C., W.Va., Ohio, and Ark.

An interesting and colorful woodsgarden plant, but must have strongly acid soil of pH 4–5, and requires protection from rodents. Pine needle and oakleaf wintercover, left in place. Propagation by seed and bulb division.

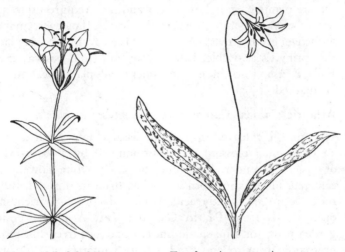

Lilium philadelphicum   *Erythronium americanum*

Common Fawnlily; Yellow Adderstongue; Troutlily; Dogtooth Violet (*Erythro'nium america'num*)

This is a low, perennial, lily-like plant rising by a thread-like underground stem from a very deeply buried bulb-like root. There are 2 brown-mottled basal leaves, from between which rises the smooth 6 to 12 inch stalk, bearing a single nodding, golden, bell-shaped flower about 1 to 2 inches long. Blossoms in early spring. Fruit an oblong capsule. Abundant in wet,

[65]

open, deciduous woods and thickets, in very deep humus-rich loam, from N.S., Ont., and Minn. south to Fla. and Ark. *Erythronium albi'dum* has white blossoms, prefers neutral soil, and is common in the midwest.

Fawnlilies are very desirable in wet, semi-shaded spots with rich moderately acid soil of pH 5–6; but their deep roots make them exceedingly difficult to transplant. An excellent method is to select in late April a square foot or so of ground on which several of the plants are blooming, excavate one or two near-by roots carefully to determine their bulb depth, mark the location of the clump precisely, and then in late August transplant the whole clump to your garden, being very certain that you have dug below the bulb-like roots. Once established, troutlilies multiply rapidly by root offshoots and seed; but immature plants have only one leaf and may require up to 5 or 6 years before blooming. Even the leaves, however, make an attractive groundcover. A leafy wintercover, left in place in the spring, is desirable. Little protection from pests is needed. Foliage disappears in late summer, and plant locations must be marked.

Atlantic Camas; Camas-Lily (*Camas'sia esculen'ta*)

Has grass-like leaves in a tight, basal clump, with a smooth 12 to 24 inch blossom stalk surmounted by a loose cylinder of ½-inch lavender, light-blue, or rarely white flowers, gold-centered. Flowers in April and May. Fruit in capsules. Bulbous root. Occurs in slightly acid to neutral (pH 6–7) rich soil in open woods from Pa. to Ga. and Tex. A highly desirable garden plant for semi-shade under deciduous trees, but requires protection from rodents, and a leafy wintercover. Propagation by bulbs and seeds.

LILY OF THE VALLEY FAMILY (*Convalla'riaceae*)

This is a most useful and interesting family, especially from the woodsgardener's point of view. Practically all of its members native to the northern states are easily transplanted, tolerant of cultivation, adapt themselves readily to a considerable variety of soils, and multiply with gratifying rapidity. Most of the species are locally common, and the serious amateur need have few qualms in collecting them.

In all species the main stem is underground, varying from short and thick to very long and slender. Propagation is principally by extension of these underground stems. Plant heights vary from a couple of inches to several feet. Fruit of all species is berry-like, usually dark blue or red.

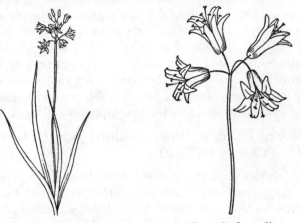

Camassia esculenta   *Clintonia borealis*

Beadlily; Yellow Clintonia (*Clinto'nia bored'lis*)

This interesting groundcover plant has 1 to 4 (usually 3) short-stemmed, oval, shiny-green, slightly fuzzy leaves, 4 to 12 inches long, springing from a stem that rises to about ground level from a rather slender rootstock. Flowers usually appear in late May or early June, and last for two weeks or more. The slender blossom stalk rises from a leaf base to a height of 6 to 15 inches, and at the top bears a loose cluster of from 2 to 7 greenish-yellow lily-like flowers about ½ to ¾ inch long. Fruit is a bead-like, dark-blue berry, ripening in September, and said to be somewhat poisonous.

The yellow beadlily is very common in shady, moist woods and thickets from Newfoundland and Manitoba to N.C. and Wis. In rough country it prefers a northeast exposure. Although it grows most luxuriantly in deep, damp, cold, hardwood leafmold, it sometimes forms a solid mat in an almost soil-less shallow depression on top of a large boulder; and in such instances the whole sheet of plants can simply be rolled up, transported, and laid down on suitable soil in your garden

—all without perceptible interruption of growth.

Beadlilies make attractive groundcover for the shadier and moister parts of your woodsgarden but, because of their trailing-root system, are usually rather difficult to transplant. If they are to flourish, they must have rich, very acid leafmold through which their delicate underground rootstocks can readily penetrate, and must be given a generous supply of water. Wintercover should be a fairly thick coating of oak leaves, left on the ground to decompose the following summer. Clintonias require an average amount of pest protection, especially against slugs and snails. They are usually propagated by dividing underground runners, but may also be readily grown from seed planted outdoors in the fall. Optimum pH 4–5.

Speckled Beadlily; White Beadlily; White Clintonia (*Clinto'nia umbellula'ta*)

This species of clintonia is more southern in its range (N.Y. to Tenn.) and has more and smaller (often spotted) white flowers and more pubescent leaves. Fruit is blackish. Its habitat is generally similar to that of the yellow-flowered species, but it prefers a somewhat less acid soil and does not need so cool or wet a location. It is therefore readily cultivatable. Optimum pH 5–6.

Solomonplume; False Solomonseal (*Smilaci'na racemo'sa*)

When growing under favorable circumstances this rather common solomonplume has a strong, unbranched, arching stem 2 to 3 feet long, bearing many alternate sessile, ribbed, oval, acuminate leaves finely pubescent underneath. Plume-like spikes of white flowers are borne at the ends of the stalks in late spring, and by September have given place to currant-like bunches of aromatic, edible, red berries. Rootstocks are fairly large and fleshy, and marked with the scars of former stems.

Although found most flourishingly in the deep, humus-rich soil of moist deciduous woods and thickets, this plant may grow, in a somewhat stunted form, in the drier, shallower, neutral soil of more open spaces. False solomonseal makes a fine plant for woodsgardens. It does well in fairly strong sun as well as rather dense shade and can adapt itself to a variety of soils. Multiplication through extension of the rootstocks may

[68]

be rapid, and the plants are resistant to pests and diseases. It is most effective in clumps of six or more stalks. Range: Eur. and northern N.A., south in mountains to Ga. and Mo. Optimum pH 5.0–6.0.

Propagation is by rootstock division and by seed. We have had best results in humus-rich garden soil of pH 5.0.

Smilacina racemosa

Starry Solomonplume (*Smilaci'na stella'ta*)

This species somewhat resembles the larger solomonplume; but its stem is stiffer and more vertical, its blossoms fewer and larger, its leaves darker green, and its berries at first green with black stripes and then dark bronze or almost black. Its underground stems are long and slender. Blooms in late spring and early summer. Range: same as *Smilaci'na racemo'sa*.

The starry solomonplume is a boon to the wildflower gardener, for it is abundant and propagates rapidly in a considerable variety of soils and locations. Even its natural habitat is varied—thickets, moist meadows, stream banks, the edges of swamps, woods, and sand dunes. We did not consciously introduce this species into our garden; but some ten summers ago a single plant made its appearance fortuitously under a clump of gray birch. It spread and spread; was started in another garden and spread again; was given away to populate other gardens; and still flourishes like the proverbial green bay tree. Yet for all its prolific hardiness it is a pretty, dark green

[69]

thing, with lovely blossoms and interesting fruit.

Propagation is by rootstock division and by seed. In some cases this plant increases so rankly that it must be ruthlessly pulled up. A 2-inch oakleaf wintercover is desirable—but by no means necessary—and may be left in place the following spring. We have had very fine results in both dry humus-rich woods loam of pH 5.0 to 5.5 and in good garden soil of pH 6.0.

Beadruby; False Lily of the Valley
(Maian'themum canaden'se)

This beautiful little plant, one of the most characteristic northeastern woodsflowers, is only 3 to 6 inches tall, but makes up in numbers what it lacks in size. The thin upright stalk, bearing only 2 or 3 leaves and surmounted by a tight plume of tiny white flowers, springs from a tangled mass of long, delicate underground stems which spread far and wide through the pure leafmold just below the surface leaves or needles of almost every patch of New England woodland. The flowers appear early in the spring and give place to ruby-colored bead-like berries which persist—unless eaten—till snowfall.

The beadruby ranges from Newfoundland to Northwest Territory and south to N.C., Tenn., Iowa, and S.D. It pokes up through the needle-carpet of dense pine groves, crams

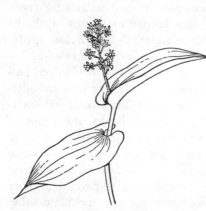

Maianthemum canadense　　　*Disporum lanuginosum*

cracks in shaded granite ledges, forms blankets over woods boulders, clothes the bases of rotting stumps and living trees, blankets springy places, and forces its way among the grass and sphagnum at bog margins. It prefers strongly acid humus-rich soil with a pH of 4-5.

The false lily of the valley should be the most omnipresent feature of your woodsgarden. Plant it at the bases of trees and stumps, in shady rock crevices, along the edges of your paths, and anywhere else you can find a place for it. Make the most of it!

This plant usually increases rapidly without any aid, but it can be propagated easily from root cuttings and seed. Wintercover, of needles or oak or beech leaves, should be provided.

Hairy Fairybells (*Dis'porum lanugino'sum*)

This plant somewhat resembles the solomonseals, but its 1 to 2½ foot stalk is branched, with terminal single or paired greenish-white bell-shaped flowers about ¾ inch long. Leaves are sessile, more narrowly ovate, and finely pubescent. Blossoms appear in late spring, and the fruit is a red berry. Habitat is neutral or moderately acid humus-rich soil in deciduous or mixed wooded areas, from Ont. to Ga. and Tenn.

Fairybells is a charming wildflower, altogether suitable for cultivation. Propagation is by seed, division, or root cuttings. Seeds should be planted when ripe. Oak or beech leaf wintercover may be left in place in the spring. Acid tolerance range is wide, about from pH 5-7, with optimum usually about pH 5.5.

Rosy, or Sessile-Leaf, Twistedstalk (*Strep'topus ro'seus*)

This is a relative of the solomonseals; but its 12 to 30-inch, minutely hairy stems are branched, have alternate sessile leaves and 1 or 2 small rose-colored flowers hanging under the stalk from the leaf axils. Blossoms appear in the late spring and give rise to red berries about ¼ inch in diameter. This plant, sometimes known as rosybells, ranges from Newfoundland and Manitoba to Ga. and Mich., and is a native of cool, moist woods with moderately acid humus-rich soil.

The rosy twistedstalk is an interesting plant for your garden if you can give it plenty of shade, rich soil, and water. Multiplication is by both root division and seed. pH 5–6, with optimum probably about pH 5.5. An oak or beech leaf winter-cover is desirable.

Streptopus roseus

Claspleaf Twistedstalk (*Strep'topus amplexifo'lius*)

This species closely resembles the rosy form, but its stems are somewhat more twisted, its leaves clasp the stem and are definitely whitish beneath, and its flowers are greenish-white. Range, habitat, soil acidity, and cultivation are substantially the same as for *Strep'topus ro'seus.*

Small, or Hairy, Solomonseal (*Polygona'tum biflo'rum*)

The hairy solomonseal is distinguished by its zigzag arched stalks from 1 to 3 feet tall, leaves that are pale and downy underneath, and greenish-white flowers hanging in pairs from the leaf axils. Range is from southern Canada to S.C. and Tenn., and west to Minn. It prefers dry woods and acid soil.

This solomonseal has done well in our gardens, single stalks quickly increasing to dense clumps. Its culture and propagation are substantially the same as those of the great solomonseal described below. A rather deep wintercover of pine needles or oak leaves is desirable and may be left in place in the spring. Although this plant tolerates considerable variations in soil acidity, it has flourished for us at pH 4.5 to 5.5.

[72]

Polygonatum biflorum

Great Solomonseal (*Polygona′tum commuta′tum*)

This plant grows to a height of 4 or 5 feet from a dense clump of large, fleshy rootstocks. Alternate, oval, heavily veined, sessile, bright green leaves spring horizontally from the upper two-thirds of the stalk; and nodding greenish-white tubular flowers, ¾ inch long, hang in clusters of 2 to 8 from the base of each leaf. Blooming is in June, the blossoms persist for about two weeks, and the ensuing bluish berries are ripe by the end of September. It is from the signet-shaped rootstock scars of this genus that the whole group of 'solomonseal' plants derives its name.

This conspicuous and beautiful plant is distributed through much of the eastern half of the U.S., and extends northeastward to N.H. and Ont. Its preferred habitat is moist, shady woodlands and thickets along streams and on bottomlands; and, although it is usually found in rich, neutral soil, it thrives also under mildly alkaline or acid conditions. It tolerates soils ranging from pH 4.0 to 7.5, but thrives best at from pH 5.0 to 6.5

Very few plants are more desirable than this in a woodland garden. It is big and showy, grows luxuriantly in partial shade,

[73]

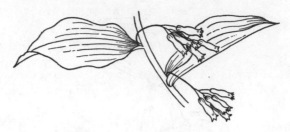

Polygonatum commutatum

forms dense masses which sometimes blanket several square yards with hundreds of close-packed stalks, tolerates wide variations in soil and water, seems almost immune to pests and diseases, and multiplies rapidly. Ten years ago we saw a clump of these big solomonseals growing in a cinder heap by the roadside, gave the owner a dollar for about a dozen rootstocks, and scattered them through our two small gardens. Today we have at least five hundred shoots scattered in shady and semishady spots all over our place, and have also given away hundreds. We have found the plant particularly effective as a background and grouped around clumps of gray birch.

The plants multiply by vigorous growth of the rootstocks, but they can be readily propagated from seed planted in an outdoor bed in the fall.

Giant Solomonseal (*Polygona'tum ma'jus gigante'um*)

This is a gorgeous plant for woodsgardens, and its general appearance, range, habitat, and cultivation are much the same as those of the great solomonseal. Its arching stalks may be 8 or more feet tall, and the pendant blossom clusters may contain up to 15 flowers each. pH 6.0–7.5

TRILLIUM FAMILY (*Trillia'ceae*)

The trilliums are a fairly large family of wild perennials with some 30 or 40 species native to North America and eastern Asia. The group is characterized by a single stem having at the top a whorl of 3 leaves and a single conspicuous flower. The flowers have 3 green sepals, 3 showy petals, 6 stamens, and a 3-celled ovary. The fruit is a many-seeded berry. Roots are tuberous. All prefer moist, fertile soil and at least partial shade.

Propagation is by seed and division; but the seeds may require two years to germinate, and the seedlings another two or three years before blooming. Soil requirements vary from slightly alkaline to very acid. Habitats may be sunlit or shady, wet or relatively dry.

There are about 25 to 30 species and sub-species native to the U.S. Several species of trilliums are commonly called wake-robin or birthroot.

A somewhat non-typical member of the family is the Indian cucumber root, in which there is a whorl of 6 leaves about half-way up the stem.

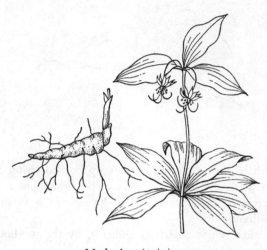

Medeola virginiana

Indian Cucumber-Root (*Mede'ola virginia'na*)

This drab cousin of the wake-robin is a slender, erect, unbranched plant from 12 to 30 inches high, woolly, and bearing a whorl of 5 to 9 pointed-oval leaves about halfway up its stem, at the apex of which is a trillium-like group of (nearly always) 3 leaves from the base of which springs a group of 2 to 9 small yellow flowers. Blossoms open in late May or June; and the purple huckleberry-like fruit ripens in September.

The cucumber root is common over most of the northeastern U.S., ranging from N.S. and Ont. to Fla., Tenn., and

Minn. It occurs abundantly, though inconspicuously, in deciduous and mixed woods and thickets, both moist and dry—though it prefers plenty of both moisture and shade, with acid, humus-rich soil of pH 4–5.

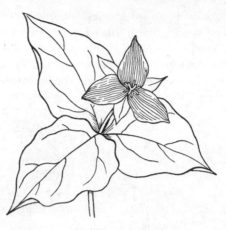

Trillium erectum

As with trilliums, propagation is by both division and seed. The perennial rootstock is 1 to 3 inches long, has a definitely cucumberous taste, and is said to have been a favorite tidbit of the Indians.

Cultivation is not especially difficult, by the methods applicable to the painted wake-robin.

Purple Trillium, Red Trillium, Wake Robin, or Birthroot (*Tril'lium erec'tum*)

This is a relatively large and conspicuous plant, with stout 8 to 16 inch stems, each topped by 3 broadly ovate, dark green, nearly sessile leaves 2 to 6 inches long. The stems rise from short, stout, scarred rootstocks, and may occur individually or in clumps of 20 or more. The flowers are single, vary from dark purplish-red to pink, are ill-smelling, and arise from the leaf whorls on stems 1 to 4 inches long. Some freakish plants bear reddish-yellow, greenish, or even white flowers. In different parts of its range the plants bloom from early May to July. Fertilization is usually by the big green fleshfly (*Lucilia cami-*

[76]

cina), which is attracted by the meaty color and odor of the flowers. Fruit is a reddish, six-lobed berry up to an inch long. Common in rather wet, cool woods and thickets, in humus-rich acid soil of pH 4.5 to 6.0. It thrives in deep hardwood leafmold; and we have seen robust plants poking up through nearly a foot of rotted sawdust at an abandoned millsite. Range: N.S. and Ont. to N.C. and Tenn.

Purple trilliums are rather easy to cultivate, and do well in humus-rich soil in full or moderate shade. Propagation is by root division and seed, the latter being easy to accomplish if the seeds are planted soon after the fruits ripen, and are left outdoors during the winter. Or the fruits may just be buried in the leafmold near the base of the parent plant, and left to their own devices.

Pest control is not difficult, though poison must be put out regularly for slugs and snails. Disease has not bothered plants in our gardens. A 2-inch layer of oak or beech leaves furnishes ideal winter protection, and should be left in place to decompose the following summer. Optimum soil acidity about pH 5.0.

Snow* or White Trillium; Large-Flowered Wake Robin
(*Tril'lium grandiflo'rum*)

This beautiful trillium resembles the purple-flowered species, except that the leaves are light green and the flowers large, white, and odorless. Blooms in May and June; the flowers last for a full month, becoming rosy-hued as they mature. Fruits and seeds resemble those of the purple trillium, but are somewhat smaller.

The snow trillium is locally abundant in open woods and thickets, preferring ravines and wooded slopes with humus-rich soil, which may be either neutral or moderately acid—pH 6–7. Range: Que. to Ont., and south to N.C., Mo., and Minn. It is the easiest of the trilliums to cultivate, thriving even in good soil and light shade among domestic plants. We placed it in our wildflower garden eleven years ago, and it has increased fully tenfold. Propagation and care are generally the

---

* The appellation 'snow' is perhaps more appropriate for *Trillium nivale*, the dwarf trillium, which is not only snow-white but sometimes blooms while the ground is still covered with snow.

the same as for its purple cousin. Good plants to naturalize
with it are the several solomonseals and the lady and Christmas ferns. With us optimum soil acidity is about pH 6.0.

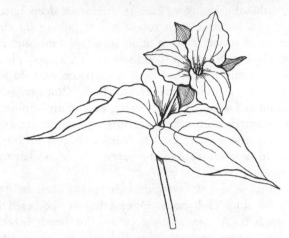

Trillium grandiflorum

Nodding Wake Robin or Trillium (*Tril'lium cer'nuum*)

A wet-ground woods plant, with all the typical trillium characteristics. It has slender stems 8 to 18 inches high, pale-green
sessile or nearly sessile leaves, wavy at the edges; and its single
rather small drooping white flowers hang almost out of sight

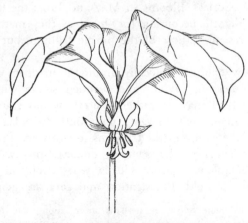

Trillium cernuum

under the leaves. Blooms appear in late May, and the relatively large, ovoid, reddish-purple berries ripen in September. Range: Newfoundland to Manitoba, and south to Ga. and Mo.

Easy to transplant and cultivate, but should have rich, moldy, moderately acid soil, considerable shade, and plenty of moisture. A single plant, brought into our garden nine years ago, now includes more than a dozen flourishing stalks. Care is generally similar to that for the purple trillium, except that maple leaves make an ideal wintercover. Slugs and snails seem to constitute its only enemies. Optimum pH 5.0–6.0.

Dwarf, or Snow, Trillium (*Tril'lium niva'le*)

This dwarf, early-blooming, white-flowered species prefers wooded slopes and rocky ledges with neutral soil. It is not native to New England, its range being from Pa. to Ky. and Neb.

Trillium nivale

However, one of these little trilliums appeared, uninvited, in our garden half a dozen years ago. It still blooms early every spring, but has not increased and does not seem at all robust. One year the stalk of this plant was accidentally broken almost through shortly after the blossom appeared; but a twig-and-scotchtape splint held it upright and healthy till fall, and the following year it bloomed as usual.

Because the dwarf trillium thrives best in neutral soil, of pH 7.0, it should be very lightly top-dressed (under the ground-litter) with garden lime each spring and fall.

[79]

Painted Trillium (*Tril'lium undula'tum*)

This rather common northern trillium has a slender stalk, 8 to 16 inches high, with 3 smooth-stemmed, waxy, bluish-green ovate leaves 3 to 6 inches long. The flowers, white with pinkish-purple markings, are borne above the leaves on upright or curved stems 1 to 2½ inches long. Blossoms usually appear late in May; and by early September the brilliant red fruits, which may be nearly an inch long, have matured.

The painted trillium thrives in the deep, very acid, humus-rich soil of moist, cool, sandy woodlands, and in cultivation is not tolerant of markedly different conditions. Range: N.S. and Ont., south to Ga., Mo., and Wis. Care and propagation are about the same as for the preceding two species except that protection from mice must be given. Optimum pH 4–5.

Trillium undulatum

Goldstar Grass (*Hypox'is hirsu'ta*)

This dainty little member of the amaryllis family is a grass-like plant with hairy leaves and ¾-inch golden star-shaped flowers. Seeds are in small capsules. Blooms May to June. Rich, very acid loam (pH 4–5) in open woods and in fields from Me. to Fla. and Tex. A good garden plant. Propagation by division. Culture easy, with no special care.

Hypoxis hirsuta

ORCHID FAMILY (*Orchida'ceae*)

Only two or three other families of flowering plants exceed the orchids in number of species. All are perennial herbs and are divided into two groups: (1) terrestrials, which grow in the ground, and (2) epiphytes, which perch on trees.

Orchid fruits are capsules that usually open by three lengthwise splits, through which innumerable minute seeds—the smallest known—are liberated. These seeds are usually slow and difficult to germinate, and seedlings often take several years to mature. But the roots of terrestrial orchids are usually fleshy, bulbous, or tuberous, and production cf new individuals from them takes place freely by division.

There are at least 150 species of orchids native to the United States and Canada, and some of them have extremely extensive ranges. Many of the northern forms are suitable for domestication and 25 are described in the following pages.

Pink Ladyslipper; Pink Moccasinflower
(*Cypripe'dium acau'le*)

The pink ladyslipper is one of our largest and most showy native orchids, and is still rather plentiful even quite near cities. It has two dark-green leaves, which spring directly from the ground and are 4 to 8 inches long, ovate, veined, and hairy.

[81]

Cypripedium acaule

The bare flower-stem stands upright between the leaves, is from 6 to 18 inches long, and at its apex bears a single pink-and-brown slipper-shaped bloom. Flowers from late May to early June.

The pink ladyslipper flourishes only in very acid soil in dryish hardwood, evergreen, and mixed woodlands. It prefers deep leafmold, though it often does well in a very thin layer of rich loam on sand or clay subsoil. On Cape Ann it grows luxuriantly on or at the base of shaded granite ledges in soil derived largely from decomposed granite rock, pine needles, and hardwood leaves; and elsewhere it has occasionally been found growing on hummocks in wet bogs (Wherry). The fleshy roots radiate almost horizontally from 6 to 12 inches from the base of the stalk, usually only 2 to 3 inches below the surface, and are frequently in close contact with underlying fragments of granite. Range: Newfoundland to Manitoba, and south to N.C., Tenn., and Minn.

All our native orchids take elaborate precautions against self-fertilization; and that the delightful shapes and colors of ladyslipper blossoms are highly functional is interestingly indicated by Moldenke, who writes:

The lip [of the moccasin flower] is somewhat obovoid, folded inward above, and has a fissure down its front. To this fissure lead scores of veins of deeper color which thus serve as the signposts [or 'nectar guide'] for the visiting insect. Insects' eyes are especially sensitive to changes in the intensity of color and these nectar guides of the moccasin flower (as of most other flowers which possess them) have their color of continually increasing intensity as the fissure is approached. They thus lead the visitor to the only spot where the slipper can be entered. Only larger insects are strong enough to open the 'door' and enter the flower. After entering, the 'door' closes behind the visitor, and it cannot be opened from the inside.

Blanchan describes the intricate mechanism of this flower as follows: 'The fissure down the front . . . is not so wide but that a bee must use some force to push against its elastic sloping sides and enter a large banquet chamber where he* finds generous entertainment secreted among the fine white hairs in the upper part. Presently he has feasted enough. Now one can hear him buzzing about inside, trying to find a way out of the trap. Toward the two little gleams of light through apertures at the end of a passage beyond the nectary hairs he at length finds his way. Narrower and narrower grows the passage until it would seem as if he could never struggle through; nor can he until his back has rubbed along the sticky, overhanging stigma, which is furnished with minute, rigid, sharply pointed papillae, all directed forward, and placed there for the express purpose of combing out the pollen he has brought from another flower on his back or head. The imported pollen having been safely removed, he still has to struggle on toward freedom through one of the narrow openings, where an anther almost blocks his way. As he works outward, this anther, drawn downward on its hinge, plasters his back with yellow granular pollen as a parting gift, and away he flies to another ladyslipper to have it combed out by the sticky stigma . . . Sometimes the largest bumblebees, either unable or unwilling to get out by the legitimate route, bite their way to liberty . . . But when unable to get out by fair means, and too bewildered to escape by foul, the large bee must sometimes perish miserably in his gorgeous prison.'

Wild cypripedium plants of this and other species can be safely dug up, transported long distances, and re-established in your garden, even when in full bloom. Take some extra soil with each plant and use it generously around the roots in the new location. In the case of the pink ladyslipper precautions must be taken to keep the soil strongly acid, for the plant simply will not thrive unless this soil acidity is maintained.

The seeds of all orchids are dust-fine, and the amateur

* The bees that gather nectar and do most of the pollinating are usually females.

[83]

gardener cannot hope to grow plants from them. Fortunately, however, the fleshy, tuberous or bulbous roots of our northern sorts each year form buds—sometimes several—from which new plants grow the following spring. In vigorous plants, this increase may double the number of stalks in a year. The resulting clusters can be successfully divided in September or October. Do not set the plants too deep—have the bud top just below the surface.

All ladyslippers are subject to fungus blight, which first spots and then gradually kills the leaves. Blight protection should be started as soon as the leaves unfold and be continued till early fall. Snails and slugs also attack the plants, often cutting off blossoms as they open. A special kind of poisoned cereal (obtainable from garden-supply stores) placed under a leaf or chip near the base of each plant will give ample protection against these pests.

On even the most flourishing plants the leaves dry up in October or early November. Winter protection should consist of a shallow layer of new-fallen pine needles and a cover of hardwood leaves—about ½ inch of needles and 1 or 2 inches of oak or beech leaves. This cover should not be removed in the spring. A light dressing of pulverized cow or sheep manure, plus a level tablespoonful each of ammonium sulphate and 20 per cent superphosphate, will furnish both the nourishment and acid to give the plants a good spring start; and a similar dressing in early July will aid in the formation of root buds. Optimum pH 4.0 to 4.5.

The flowers of this ladyslipper vary from dark crimson-pink to clear white, the white form being rare over most of the plant's range. Cultivation is the same for all the color phases.

Ramshead Ladyslipper (*Cypripe'dium arieti'num*)

A small plant, resembling the white ladyslipper in size and general appearance, but having a weirdly shaped single red-and-white bloom. Blossoms in May and June. Range: Que. to Manitoba, Mass., N.Y., and Minn.

A very rare plant of cold and damp northern woods and cedar swamps. Not to be collected unless you can give it dense cool shade, moderately acid leafmold, and lots of water.

[84]

Cypripedium arietinum

Small Yellow Ladyslipper (*Cypripe'dium parviflo'rum*)

This ladyslipper has a stem from 8 inches to 1½ feet high, with dark-green, heavily veined, ovate, alternate, clasping leaves. At the top of the stem are a pointed leaf and a single flower having a yellow lip and 3 long, narrow, bronze-colored sepals. Blooms April to June. Flowers fragrant. Range: northeastern Canada and northeastern states.

The small yellow ladyslipper prefers deep humus in rich woods and dense thickets; but when domesticated it is somewhat tolerant of varied growing conditions. For best results it should have hardwood humus, plenty of moisture, and moderately acid (pH 5–6) soil. It is subject to fungus damage, and slugs delight in nipping off the newly opened blossoms. Propagation is by division of clumps growing from root buds.

Large Yellow Ladyslipper
(*Cypripe'dium parviflo'rum pubes'cens*)

This species is similar to the small yellow ladyslipper in appearance, except that it averages considerably larger; but its habitat and cultivation are very different from those of the smaller form. Its range extends much further south (N.S. to Ont. and south to Ala., Minn., and Neb.), and its habitat is more varied. Dr. Edgar T. Wherry has recently written us that '. . the [large] yellow ladyslipper is the easiest of all orchids to grow.

[85]

I have one 35 years old, and have heard of them reaching 100 years. One reason is that it has no restricted pH range, although the optimum is presumably around pH 6 (might be stated as 5–7).' Blooms usually in June. Requires vigilant protection from fungi, slugs, and snails.

The large yellow ladyslipper can be purchased from most wildflower dealers, and should certainly be one of the first inhabitants of your garden.

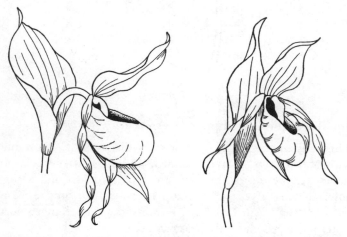

Cypripedium parviflorum pubescens   *Cypripedium candidum*

White Ladyslipper (*Cypripe'dium can'didum*)

One of the rarest and smallest of the 'slippers, its maximum height being only about 12 inches. There are from 3 to 5 veined and pointed leaves on each rather stiffly erect stalk, at the top of which is 1 (rarely 2) white, moccasin-shaped bloom. It is found in marly bogs, low meadows, and, occasionally, in sphagnum bogs. Flowers in May and June. Is said to increase quickly under favorable conditions, sometimes accumulating into clumps of 50 or more stalks. Range: N.Y. and Ont. to Minn., Mo., and Ky.

This orchid is not only rare but difficult for the amateur to grow. Therefore, its cultivation should be attempted only if moderate shade, slightly alkaline or neutral humus-rich muck, and plenty of water are available. It will require protection against disease, snails, slugs, insects, and rodents. A

[86]

level tablespoonful of garden lime, scattered each spring among the litter over the plant, will prevent the soil from becoming acid. Optimum pH 6.5 to 7.5.

Showy Ladyslipper (*Cypripe'dium regi'nae*)

This is our largest and showiest native orchid. It has a strong hairy stalk 1½ to 3 feet tall, with several alternate clasping hairy leaves. Flowers are usually 1 or 2 in number (occasionally 3) to a stalk, from 1½ to 2 inches long, and of beautifully contrasting colors—with petals and sepals white, and mocassin-shaped lip white flooded with rose or crimson. Blooms rather late as compared to other ladyslippers—from late June to August.

The showy ladyslipper is a plant of swamps, bogs, and very wet woods. It requires wet, slightly acid muck, and a good bit of sunshine. We have found it flourishing in an almost bottomless sphagnum bog and growing even more luxuriantly among the brush and ferns in an open spot on the bank of a mountain brook. Range: Newfoundland to Ont., and south to Ga., Minn., and Mo.

If you decide to bring this rare and beautiful orchid to your garden, give it a semi-shaded location, deep humus-rich muck,

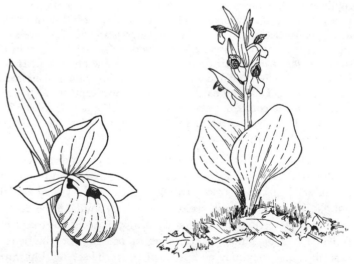

Cypripedium reginae   *Orchis spectabilis*

[87]

and lots of water. Protect it from snails, slugs, and leaf blight. Each fall give it a generous cover of mixed hardwood leaves, some of which may the following spring be left in place to rot and replenish the humus. Optimum pH 5–7.

Showy Orchis (*Or'chis specta'bilis*)

As its name implies, this attractive purple-and-white orchid can be an eye-pulling feature of your woodsgarden. It is a stocky plant, with 2 heavy, glossy green leaves at the ground and a fleshy 6 to 12 inch stalk rising from a short rootstock with many thick roots. Sometimes the leaves have a 'clammy' feel caused by the exudation of moisture. The stalk bears 3 to 10 showy purple-and-white blossoms, which may appear late in April or May and persist through June. Range: N.B. to Ont., and south to Ga., Ky., Mo., Minn., and N.D.

Of the reproduction of this plant, Moldenke writes:

The showy orchis is the only one of our species known to be dependent upon individuals of one sex of an insect for pollination. It blooms before the male bumblebees are hatched, and only the females are flying. Furthermore, only the females of these insects have the smooth cheeks required to effect pollination of this flower. As the insect visitor pushes her head into the center of the flower to sip the nectar at the base of the spur, she presses against and ruptures a thin membrane covering a pouch containing the two sticky disks. Instantly upon contact these disks cement themselves to her bare cheeks. As she withdraws her head the disks are taken along and to each is attached a pollen mass on a perpendicular stalk. Contact with the air produces a remarkable physiologic change in this stalk, which contracts and assumes a horizontal plane before the bee has had time to back out of the flower and fly to the next one. When she enters the next flower, the two pollinia will be held horizontally on her cheeks in just the proper position to strike and adhere to the sticky stigma waiting to receive them.

The showy orchis is an inhabitant of rich, moist woods in moderately acid hardwood leafmold. If these conditions are reproduced in your garden, this grand little plant may actually double in number each year, from root buds. However, it requires protection from snails, slugs, insects, disease, and rodents. A 1 or 2 inch wintercover of oak and beech leaves is desirable, and they may be left in place in the spring. Optimum pH 5.5 to 6.5.

[88]

Satyr, Whitefringe Orchid (*Habena'ria vir'idis bractea'ta*)

Found both in the open around swamps and in cold damp woods, this plant has a leafy stalk 1 or 2 feet high topped by a 2 to 5 inch spike of small greenish-white flowers. Blooms May to August. Requires acid, humus-rich soil. Range: Eur., Asia and northern N.A., south to N.C., Minn., and Wash.

This is a difficult and not very rewarding orchid to cultivate. It requires exact reproduction of its natural surroundings and is attacked by several pests and diseases. Optimum pH 4.0 to 4.5.

Roundleaf Orchid (*Habena'ria rotundifo'lia*)

A small one-leaf, white-rose-and-purple-flowered inhabitant of cold northern woods and bogs. Definitely not suitable for cultivation.

Hooker Orchid (*Habena'ria hook'eri*)

In this interesting but unspectacular woods orchid both the two fleshy, shining, dark-green, broadly ovate ground-level leaves and the stout 8 to 15 inch flowering stalk spring directly from the tuberous underground stem. The yellowish-green flowers, arranged loosely around the upper two-thirds of the stalk, are about ½ to ¾ inch long, and are found from June to Sept. Range: N.S. and Que. to Pa., Minn., and Iowa.

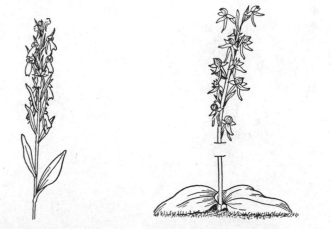

Habenaria viridis bracteata   *Habenaria hookeri*

Hooker orchid flourishes in mountains and foothills in dense, cool, damp woods—either coniferous or deciduous—associated with such acid-loving plants as painted trilliums and clintonias; and its cultivation should be about the same as that of those two plants. It multiplies by buds from the underground stem. An oak or beech leaf wintercover is desirable, and may be left in place in the spring. Optimum pH 4–5.

Padleaf Orchid (*Habena'ria orbicula'ta*)

In general appearance this orchid resembles *Habena'ria hook'eri,* but its blossom stalk is longer (up to 24 inches) and slenderer. Its two broad, green leaves are silvery beneath and lie flat on the ground, and its whitish flowers are considerably larger than those of the preceding species. Its habitat and cultivation are much the same, except that it prefers mixed deciduous forests where soil conditions are only moderately acid. Range: Newfoundland to Alaska, south to S.C., W.Va., and Nev. to Wash. Optimum pH 5–6.

Yellow Fringe-Orchid (*Habena'ria cilia'ris*)

This is a tall and spectacular orchid with a 1½ to 3 foot blossom stalk bearing large leaves near its base, smaller leaves and bracts (scale-like leaves) higher up, and a spike of brilliantly yellow or orange flowers at the top. Blooms July and Aug. Range: Ont. to Fla., west to Mich. and Tex.

Habenaria ciliaris   *Pogonia trianthophora*

The yellow fringe-orchid is a southern type, only rarely found in some northeastern states. It is a vigorous inhabitant of moist, open places in woods and of damp grasslands and bog margins. It is not really a woods plant, and its cultivation should not be attempted unless your garden contains just the right spot—fairly sunny and damp, with deep, humus-rich, at least slightly acid soil. Propagation is the same as for the other Habenaria orchids. A light wintercover of sphagnum, saltmarsh hay, or cranberry vines is desirable. Optimum pH 5.0 to 6.0.

Drooping Pogonia; Little-Bird Orchid
(Pogo'nia trianthoph'ora)

This is a tiny 4 to 8 inch almost leafless orchid sprouting from an underground stem or tuber and bearing a few allegedly bird-like lilac or whitish flowers on its upper stem. It is an inhabitant of neutral or slightly acid, humus-rich loam in deciduous or mixed woods. The plants die and disappear after blooming, but produce new tubers which usually remain dormant for several years.

You will have little difficulty transplanting this orchid into your garden; but you will certainly have to protect it very carefully from rodents; and, unless you have the memory of the proverbial elephant, you should keep its location well marked while it is hidden below the surface. Wintercover of oak or beech leaves, partly removed in the spring. Optimum pH 6–7.

Atlantic or Whorled Pogonia; Fiveleaf Orchid
(Pogo'nia verticilla'ta)

In this dainty little orchid a single 10 to 15 inch stem rises from a long, somewhat fleshy rootstock and at its apex bears a whorl of 5 sharply pointed sessile leaves, which are usually not fully developed when the plant blooms. The one beautiful pink-purple-and-white flower springs from the leaf whorl and is nearly erect on its short stem. An inhabitant of moist woods, low meadows, and bogs. Blooms May to June. Range: Ont. to Fla., west to Tenn., Mich., and Wis. Although difficult to transplant because of its long underground rootstocks, it can be cultivated in mixed pine and oak woods having deep, rich, strongly acid soil. Protection from pests—particularly slugs and snails—is essential. Optimum pH 4–5.

Fullcrest Pogonia (*Pogo'nia affi'nis*)

This woods pogonia, very much like that above but smaller and greenish-flowered, is both very rare and difficult to cultivate. If found, it should be left undisturbed.

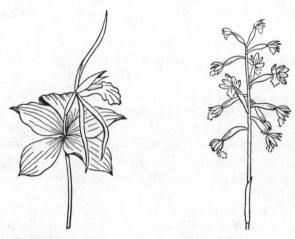

Pogonia verticillata   *Corallorrhiza maculata*

Spotted Coralroot (*Corallorrhi'za macula'ta*)

All the coralroots lack true leaves and green coloring matter. They are absolutely dependent upon soil fungi, which cluster about their coral-like rootstocks and supply them with the liquid nourishment without which they cannot live. For this reason they are extremely difficult to transplant; but occasionally they may appear in your garden, into which their seeds may have been accidentally carried. There are some five northeastern species.

The spotted or large coralroot has large bronze-scaled stalks, 8 to 15 inches tall. Flowers are numerous, ¾ inch long, with bronzy, purple and white (rarely yellowish) coloring. This orchid is found in woods with slightly acid, humus-rich soil. Range: Newfoundland and N.S. west to B.C., and south to Fla., Mo., N.M., and Calif. Optimum pH 6.0 to 6.5.

[92]

Late or Fall Coralroot (*Corallorrhi'za odontorhi'za*)

A tiny orchid, 6 to 12 inches high, with very inconspicuous purplish flowers. Grows in moderately acid woods (pH 5–6). Blossoms July to Sept. A southern species, extending north to Me., Ont., and Ill.

Early Coralroot (*Corallorrhi'za trifi'da*)

Another small and delicate plant, 6 to 12 inches tall, with greenish-yellow and purplish-white flowers. Found in deep, wet woods and swamps in soil usually only moderately acid (pH 5–6), in Eurasia; and from Newfoundland to Alaska, and south to Ga., Ohio, Mich. and Minn.

Hooded or Striped Coralroot (*Corallorrhi'za stria'ta*)

This is the largest and showiest of the group, with 18-inch stalks and purple-striped (rarely yellowish) flowers. It lives in cool woods and around swamp margins in neutral or slightly acid soil. Blooms in midsummer. Range: Que. and B.C., south to northern N.E., Mich., N.M., and Calif. Optimum pH 6–7.

Downy Rattlesnake-Plantain (*Good'yera pubes'cens*)

This, in spite of its common name, is not a plantain but a true orchid inhabiting warm, rather dry northeastern woods, usually in humus-rich acid soil under pines, hemlocks, or oaks. The flower stalk is 6 to 20 inches tall, bears numerous small white or greenish blossoms, and in general appearance closely resembles some of the ladies-tresses. The small, oval, fleshy green leaves are bunched at the base of the flower stalk and are conspicuously veined with white. Blossoms during the summer. Multiplication is by seed and by lengthening and rooting of stems at or near the ground surface. Range: Ont. and N.S., south to Fla. and Minn.

Downy rattlesnake-plantains are easy to transplant and, if given the usual protection from diseases and pests, may do very well under cultivation. There are two additional species found in New England, the Lesser (*Goodyera repens*) and Checkered (*Goodyera tesselata*). The former is not suitable for cultivation, but the latter can be handled like *Goodyera pubescens*—although it requires a damper, more acid soil.

[93]

Wintercover, preferably of pine needles, is needed, but should be removed in the spring. Propagation in the garden is by rooted sections of the creeping stems. Optimum pH 4–5.

Goodyera pubescens   *Liparis liliifolia*

Lily Twayblade (*Lip'aris liliifo'lia*)

In this exceedingly delicate little woods orchid a pair of oval, shiny, light-green leaves rises from a scaly crown above a small bulb. The blossom stem rises 6 to 12 inches and on its upper two-thirds bears a loose spike of showy purple (rarely yellow) flowers. Blooms May to June. Range: Me. to Ga. and Ala., and Minn. to Mo. Optimum pH 4–5.

Calypso (*Calyp'so bulbo'sa*)

This is one of our most delicately beautiful northern orchids. There is only one leaf, and a scaled stem rises for 3 to 7 inches above a bulb only ½ inch or less in diameter. The single bloom is 1 to 1½ inches long and colored a mixture of pink, purple, and yellow. Calypso is more partial to bogs than to woods and can be cultivated with great difficulty—and then only in wet, cold, moderately acid humus. Range: Eur., Asia, and N.A. Across Canada and south to N.E., Mich., Minn., Ariz., and Calif. Optimum pH 5–6.

[94]

Puttyroot Orchid (*Aplec'trum hyema'le*)

This is an inconspicuous, single-leaved, spring-blooming inhabitant of damp woods with deep neutral or slightly acid, humus-rich soil. The one dark-green leaf, purple on the underside, appears in the autumn, remains green throughout the winter, and withers before the plant blooms. The flowers are yellow-brown, and are borne in a cluster on the upper part of a leafless stem up to 20 inches long, in May and June. The underground growth consists of a series of connected round tubers, the putty-like contents of which give the plant its common name. Range: southern Can. and northeastern U.S., south in mountains to Ga.

Calypso bulbosa   *Aplectrum hyemale*

This little orchid is sensitive to soil change, so when transplanted it should be well surrounded with dirt from its original location. Its tubers are eagerly eaten by mice; and slugs may devour its one leaf. Even so, it is a worth-while addition to your garden. Multiplication is by the tubers. pH 6–7.

Cranefly Orchid (*Tipula'ria unifo'lia*)

In this orchid, a single leaf and a stalk 1 to 2 feet high rise from a deformed tuberous rootstock. Leaf dark green above, prominently veined, appearing in fall and withering in spring before flowers appear. The numerous bronzy flowers surround the upper half of the stalk. Blooms in July and August. Range: Mass. to Fla., Ind., and Tex.

This is a good plant for your woodland garden, and should do well in rich acid woods-compost or leafmold derived from a mixture of pine needles and oak leaves. Multiplication is by means of the extending rootstock. Rodents are fond of its tubers and must be kept away from them. Optimum pH 4–5.

Crested Coralroot (*Hexalec'tris spica'ta*)

This is not a true coralroot, but is so closely related that its habit of growth, habitat, and relation to cultivation are substantially similar to the species described above. It has a scaly stalk some 2 feet high, and a few 1-inch bronzy flowers conspicuously striped with purple. Blooms in summer and likes rather poor neutral soil on shaded rock ledges and in rocky woods. A southern plant, not reaching New England or other northern states. Transplantable and cultivatable only with great difficulty. Optimum pH 6.5 to 7.0.

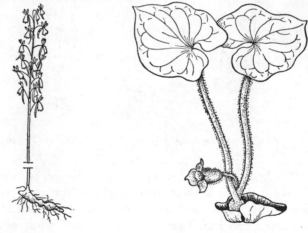

Tipularia unifolia   *Asarum canadense*

Canada Wildginger; Indian Ginger; Ginger-Root (*A'sarum canaden'se*)

Wildginger has long-stemmed dark-green, almost triangular leaves springing from fleshy rootstocks which form a crowded network on the ground in rich, moist woods. The short-

[96]

stemmed reddish-brown fleshy flowers appear at ground level before the leaves are fully grown. The whole plant is hairy. Blossoms in April and May. Range: N.B. to Man., and south to N.C., Mo. and Kan. Closely allied species or varieties range through most wooded areas of the U.S.

Of this wildginger, Moldenke writes:

Completely hidden from the view of insects flying above the leaves, the brownish purple flowers, lying on the ground or even among or beneath dead leaves and other forest litter, are attractive to gnats, small flies, and beetles, which are just then beginning to warm up and become active after spending the cold winter as maggots or grubs under dead leaves or in the bark of rotting logs. The cuplike flowers, lying among the dead leaves on the forest floor, furnish a snug warm place of refuge from the chill spring winds. When the flower first opens, only the pistil is mature, and pollen brought from older flowers is rubbed on to the sticky stigma. After pollination has been thus effected, the 12 stamens elongate and are ready to shed pollen on later insect visitors for transportation by them to younger flowers of another plant. Since only one flower is produced per plant (usually), this assures cross-fertilization and the healthier, more vigorous offspring which Charles Darwin proved result from such cross-fertilization.

The name of this plant derives from the strong gingery flavor of its rootstocks, which have almost as much bite as the tropical ginger-root of commerce. Cultivation is very easy if rich, moderately acid soil (pH 4.5–6.0), shade, and moisture are furnished. Not much affected by disease or pests. Propagated by division. Wintercover of oak or beech leaves, not removed in the spring.

Common Dutchmanspipe; Pipe-Vine (*Aristolo'chia du'rior*)

A tall-climbing perennial with long-stemmed, heart-shaped leaves and even longer-stemmed, pipe-shaped, greenish-bronze flowers. Blooms June to July. Fruit a capsule. Rocky woods, in slightly acid soil of pH 6–7, from N.E. south and west. Easy to cultivate. Propagation by root division and seed.

Common Pokeberry; Inkberry (*Phytolac'ca america'na*)

A very large herbaceous perennial plant, many-branched and reaching a height of 10 feet. Leaves large, oval, and alternate.

[97]

Spikes of small white flowers develop into bunches of purplish-black berries with ink-like juice. Open woods and thickets in poor soil, from Me. and Ont. to Bermuda, Fla., Ark., and Mex. Preferred pH, 5–6.

This is a rapidly multiplying, weedy plant and should not be admitted to the garden. The berries and roots are poisonous, but the young leafy shoots are excellent boiled like asparagus.

Firepink Silene; Red Catchfly; Fire Pink
(Sile'ne virgin'ica)

This colorful herb has a rather weak 12 to 18 inch stem, with long, narrow, opposite clasping leaves. The bright-red flowers are 5-rayed and about 1½ inches across. Blooms May to Aug. Fruit a bell-shaped capsule. On slopes and in open woods from N.Y. to Ga. and Ark. Likes rich soil of pH 5–7. Can be cultivated, but is attacked by pests and blight. Propagated by seeds. The starry silene *(Silene stellata)* is 2 to 3 feet high, erect, with sessile leaves in whorls of 4. Blossoms are white.

Aristolochia durior   *Claytonia virginica*

Virginia Spring Beauty; Narrow-Leaved Spring Beauty
(Clayto'nia virgin'ica)

These delicate, early-blooming perennial plants are as beautiful as their name implies. Their slender 6 to 12 inch stems arise from deep-buried tuberous or corm-like roots, and near the ground bear 2 narrow, opposite leaves up to 7 inches long. Several flowers are borne in a loose cluster in the upper part of the stem. They are ½ to ⅞ inch across and are white or pink, with darker veins. Fruit is a capsule.

This spring beauty is found in moist, open woods and thickets from N.S. to Sask. and south to Ga., Tex., and Mont. It tolerates a considerable variety of soils, ranging from humus-rich and moderately acid to nearly neutral garden loam.

Half a dozen years ago a spring beauty appeared gratuitously in a semi-shaded part of our garden—we never could even guess where it came from—and since then has spread and thrived. It apparently increases by both seeds and division.

Both this and the succeeding species disappear from above ground shortly after the seed capsules have ripened; and the location of each group of plants must be indicated by markers. Wintercover of oak or beech leaves, most of which should be removed very early in the spring. Not greatly subject to disease or pests. Optimum pH probably 5–6.

Carolina Spring Beauty (*Clayto'nia carolinia'na*)

This plant closely resembles the foregoing, but its leaves are shorter and wider, its stem more erect, and its flowers fewer. Its range is nearly co-extensive with the narrow-leaved species; and its cultural requirements approximately the same.

Bristly Buttercup; Hispid Buttercup
(*Ranun'culus his'pidus*)

This buttercup is found in dry woods and thickets throughout most of eastern Canada and the United States. However, any buttercup may act as a weed, so our advice is: keep this and all others out of all of your gardens—if you can! Preferred pH, 5–6.

Anemonella; Rue Anemone (*Anemonel'la thalictroi'des*)

This is a delicately beautiful, anemone-like woods plant rising to 9 inches from a perennial tuberous rootstock. At the top of the stalk is a whorl of sessile, 3-parted, dark-green leaves. Blossoms arise on delicate stems from the upper leaf-whorl, and are pinkish, lavender-tinged, or white. Blossoms from late March to early June. Usually found in fairly open deciduous woods, frequently associated with round-lobed hepaticas in moderately acid soil of pH 4–6. Range: N.H. to Ont. and Minn. and south to Fla., Tenn., and Kans.

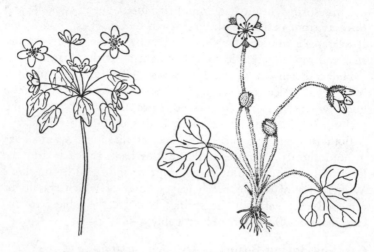

Anemonella thalictroides   *Hepatica americana*

Roundlobe Hepatica; Liverleaf (*Hepat'ica americd'na*)

This is one of our best-known wildflowers. It is a small perennial herb with fibrous roots. Blossoms are white, pink, or purple and appear very early in the spring—sometimes in March—on fuzzy 4 to 6 inch stems. The leaves grow from the heart at ground level after the plant has bloomed. They are on 3 to 6 inch hairy stems and are 3-lobed, rounded, and evergreen till the following spring. This plant likes dry, rocky, oak-grown hillsides and humus-rich, acid soil (pH 4.5–6). It is frequently associated with the rue anemone. Range: N.S., Ont., Manitoba, and Alaska south to Fla., Ark., Minn., and Iowa.

Hepaticas are favorites in the woodsgarden, where they do very well if properly cared for. Slugs, snails, and insects may attack both blossoms and leaves; and sometimes leaves are blighted. A light oak or beech leaf wintercover is desirable, but should be removed by late March or early April. Propagation is by seed, or by division in the fall.

Sharplobe Hepatica (*Hepat'ica acutilo'ba*)

Closely resembles the preceding species, but its leaf lobes are pointed and its flowers somewhat larger. Its habitat and range are very similar to those of the roundlobe hepatica, but it is rare or absent from the Atlantic coastal regions. Moreover, the sharplobe hepatica occurs only in slightly acid or neutral soil and so does not grow side-by-side with the roundlobe. Nevertheless, puzzling intermediate forms sometimes appear. Cultivation like that of *Hepatica americana*. Optimum pH 6–7.

Meadow Anemone; Canada or Round-Leaf Anemone
(*Anem'one canaden'sis*)

Attains a height of only 2 feet and is somewhat hairy. Leaves near the bottom of the stalk are long-stemmed, broader than long, and 3- to 5-pointed. Higher leaves are similar but stemless. Flowers spring on slender stems from the uppermost leaf-whorls, and are white with golden centers. Blooms April to May. Open woods, thickets, and roadsides in a considerable variety of soils, usually somewhat acid (pH 6–7). Ranges from Labrador to Assiniboine and south to Ga., Tenn., Ill., Minn., Kans., and Colo.

This anemone is just too easy to naturalize in your wild garden, and may take over completely if introduced. Keep it out—unless you are willing to confine it strictly by means of a 12-inch metal strip (see chapter iv). Even so, it may get away from you.

American Wood Anemone; Windflower
(*Anem'one quinquefo'lia*)

This is the smallest of our anemones, with a slender 4 to 8 inch stalk bearing at its base several long-stemmed, 5-parted leaves and, at its apex, a whorl of 3- to 5-parted leaves deeply and variously cut. Rootstocks are perennial, creeping, and horizontal. Flowers spring from center of leaf-whorl, are solitary and white or lavender-tinged. Blooms in April or early May. Common in wet woodlands, thickets, and along shady roadsides, frequently in the company of cinnamon, interrupted, and royal ferns. Ranges from Nova Scotia to Ga. and Tenn. Requires damp, rich, mucky, moderately acid soil (pH 5–6).

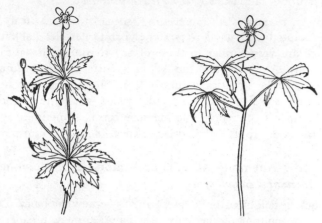

Anemone canadensis   Anemone quinquefolia

Can be readily transplanted, but usually does not bloom freely under cultivation. Propagated by spreading rootstocks and root cuttings. Disappears after blooming, so that its location must be plainly marked.

Virginia Anemone; Thimbleweed (*Anem'one virginid'na*)
This 2 to 3 foot plant is the largest of our anemones and is rather coarse and unattractive. It has stout stalks and whorls of dark-green deeply cut leaves, with long-stemmed white or greenish-white flowers rising from the top leaf-whorl. Fruit is globular and burr-like, hence one of the common names. Blooms in July. Stalk, leaf, and flower very similar to those of wood anemone, but larger and coarser. Habitat dry open woods and slopes, in rather poor moderately acid or neutral soil. Relatively free from diseases and pests. Range: Nova Scotia to Alberta, and south to S.C., Ark., and Kans.

Easily cultivated, but should be closely watched to prevent unwanted spreading. Wintercover permissible but not necessary. Optimum pH: 5.5 to 7.0.

Rock Clematis; Purple Virginsbower
(*Clem'atis verticilla'ris*)
A climbing vine up to 10 feet long, with groups of 3-parted compound leaves and 2 to 4 inches, thin-stemmed, purplish-blue, bell-shaped flowers at intervals along the stalk. Blooms

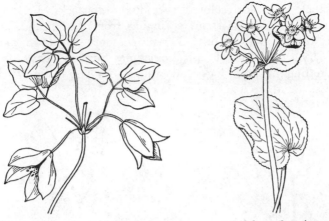

Clematis verticillaris   *Caltha palustris*

May to June. Woods, thickets, and shady rock-slides, in cool, humus-rich soil, usually of pH 6–7. Hudson's Bay and Manitoba south to Conn., Va., and Minn. A fine twining plant for a large woodsgarden. Propagation by softwood cuttings, divisions, and seeds. Subject to insects and blight. Groundcover desirable.

Common Marsh-Marigold; American Cowslip
(*Cal'tha palus'tris*)

A large perennial with thick, hollow stems, broadly heart-shaped leaves, and terminal clusters of bright-yellow, buttercup-like flowers. Blooms in May. Inhabits soaking-wet deciduous woods, streambanks, and meadows with muddy, humus-rich soil, of various reactions (pH 5–7), from Newf. to Sask. and south to S.C. & Neb.

A colorful and easy-to-grow ornament for any garden having wet, mucky soil and either full sun or light shade. Reproduced rapidly by seed and division. Requires little care other than protection—an overturned berry basket—from drying winter and early spring winds. Used as a 'pot-herb' when coming into bloom.

Common Goldthread (*Cop'tis groenlan'dica*)

This is another fine groundcover plant for the wildgarden. Its evergreen 3-lobed leaves arise on delicate stems directly from

[103]

the tangle of golden-colored threadlike rootstocks. Flowers, also borne on delicate stems springing from the ground, are white. Blooms May to July. Thrives in moist woods in cool, rich, very acid soil of pH 4–5, sometimes forming dense mats over rotting hemlock logs and stumps. Ranges from Newf. and Lab. south to Va., Tenn., Minn., and Iowa.

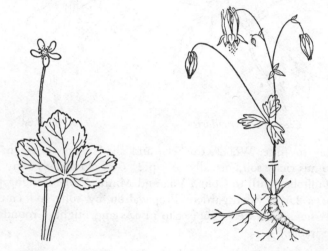

Coptis groenlandica   *Aquilegia canadensis*

Goldthread can be successfully cultivated only in a cool, moist, shady area. Wintercover of oak leaves, partly removed in the spring, is desirable. Propagated by root cuttings or seeds.

The underground stems possess astringent properties and are used medicinally.

American Columbine; Rock-Bells; Wild Columbine
(*Aquile'gia canaden'sis*)

This popular wildflower is erect and branching, with compound leaves and nodding, scarlet (rarely white or yellow) multi-spurred flowers. It is from 1 to 2 feet high, and grows in dry rocky woods and clearings, in partial shade or in full sun, and in dry soil either rich or poor. Blooms May to July. Range: Nova Scotia to North West Territory and south to Fla. and Tex. Tolerated pH range from 5.0 to 7.5; optimum 6–7.

A most satisfactory plant for the wildgarden and for many spots outside it. Requires almost no care and spreads rapidly by

[104]

seed. Its perennial rootstock goes deep into the soil and enables it to survive even the worst drouths.

Tall Larkspur (*Delphin'ium exalta'tum*)

Grows 2 to 6 feet high from a thick perennial root. The compound leaves are cut into mostly 5-toothed leaflets. Lavender or blue flowers, ¾ inches long, form a loose terminal spike. Blooms July to Aug. Mixed deciduous woods with rich slightly acid or neutral soil of pH 6–7, from Pa. and Minn. to Ala. and Neb.

Gives midsummer color and is easy to grow. Propagation by seeds and division. Semi-shade. No special care.

Cohosh Bugbane; Fairy Candles (*Cimicif'uga racemo'sa*)

This is a large, bush-like, herbaceous perennial plant, 3 to 8 feet high, with compound saw-edged leaves and long candles of tiny white, fuzzy, rank-centered flowers. Blooms in July and August. Inhabits rocky woods and woodland clearings in moderately acid (pH 5–6) loam. Range: Me. to Ga., and Ont. and Wis. to Mo.

Suitable for large gardens only. Thrives under cultivation, requiring no special care.

Delphinium exaltatum   *Cimicifuga racemosa*

Red Baneberry (*Actae'a ru'bra*)

This is an attractive perennial plant, 1 to 2 feet high, with branched stems and compound leaves. The dense globular clusters of small white flowers are borne at the upper ends of the stalks from April to early June. Fruit is a bright-red poisonous berry. Range: Labrador to Ontario and south to N.J., Pa., Neb., and S.D. Habitat: mixed woods, thickets, and shaded banks, in moderately acid to neutral soil (pH 5–7).

The red baneberry is a fine plant for the wildgarden. Propagated by root division in very early spring or fall, or by seed. Wintercover of oak or beech leaves, left in place. Optimum pH probably 5.0 to 6.0.

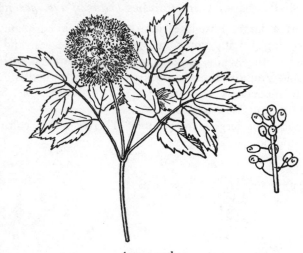

Actaea rubra

White Baneberry (*Actae'a al'ba*)

Resembles very closely the red baneberry in everything but its fruits, which are a waxy white with a black eye opposite the stem end, the berry stems being a bright red. These two species of baneberries are often found close together and their ranges and cultural requirements are substantially identical.

The fruit of this species, too, is poisonous to humans; but it disappears so fast from our garden that we suspect it actually improves the digestion of some small bird or mammal!

[106]

Goldenseal; Orange-Root (*Hydras'tis canaden'sis*)

A good groundcover plant for moist, shady, humus-rich spots in woodsgardens. Its relatively large shiny green leaves, deeply cut like those of some maples, spring from heavy orange-colored rootstocks. The inconspicuous greenish-white flower rises on a short stem from the center of the leaf in early spring, and develops into a crimson fruit.

Goldenseal prefers moist, humus-rich, slightly acid soil on north slopes; and ranges from Que. and Ont. to Ga., Mo., Minn., and Kans.

This is an easy plant to cultivate. In fact, it is grown commercially for its medicinally valuable underground stem. Beech-leaf wintercover desirable. Optimum pH 6.0 to 6.5.

Hydrastis canadensis

Mayapple; Wild Mandrake (*Podophyl'lum pelta'tum*)

The twin umbrella-like leaves of this plant rise directly from the poisonous fleshy creeping rootstock in the early spring. At first the 'umbrella' is tightly closed and shows a whitish top and light-green sides. As the stem lengthens, the pair of leaves at its top unfolds till, when the stem is almost fully developed, the single white or pinkish blossom nods below the leaves. By the end of summer the 'mayapple' has formed— an insipid, edible, yellowish fruit about an inch in diameter.

Podophyllum peltatum

Although the fruit is harmless, both the foliage and root-stocks are said to be mildly poisonous and serious illness has resulted from eating mayapple leaves as greens. Homer D. House writes:

The root is a violent purgative, resembling jalap in its action. Its popular name, Mandrake, relates it in no way to the Mandrake or Mandragora of the ancients and, notwithstanding its poisonous character it is a very respectable herb in comparison with the traditions of the Mandrake of the ancients, described as flourishing best under a gallows, with a root resembling a man in shape, uttering terrible shrieks when it was torn from the ground, and possessing the power of transforming men and beasts.

Mayapples often form dense mats in damp open maple woods, in clearings, and along roadsides, thriving in very to only slightly acid soil, of pH 4–7. They are not common in the coastal areas of N.E.

This is a fine groundcover plant for large wildgardens and for naturalizing in many other damp shady areas. It can, however, be a rank-grower which will crowd out more delicate species.

American Twinleaf (*Jefferso'nia diphyl'la*)

This interesting perennial derives its name from the fact that the single roundish leaf at the apex of each stem is divided into 2 substantially identical parts. Leaves and flower stalks both rise directly from an underground rootstock. Leaves are finely fuzzy beneath and have reached only about half their mature height—12 to 18 inches—when the plant blossoms in April or May. The flowers are on leafless stems somewhat longer than those of the leaves; and are white, flat, 8-petaled, and star-like. The fruit is an interesting capsule wih a hinged cover that pops open when the seeds are ripe—the whole fruit, with its stem, resembling a covered tobacco pipe.

Twinleaf thrives in rich, damp, open woods, in acid or neutral soil of pH 4.5–7. It ranges from Ontario to Va., Tenn., Wis., and Iowa.

A fine woodsgarden plant, requiring little protection from pests and disease. It is easily propagated from seeds or by division in the fall. A leafy wintercover is desirable and should not be removed. In the authors' gardens twinleaf does

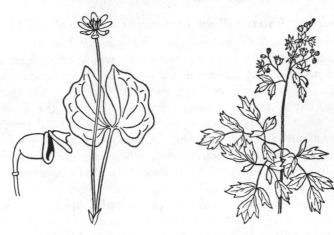

Jeffersonia diphylla   *Caulophyllum thalictroides*

best in humus-rich soil of about pH 4.5. The pipe-like seedcases are known to very few wildgardeners and therefore make interesting exhibits at garden club meetings.

[109]

Blue Cohosh (*Caulophyl'lum thalictroi'des*)

The blue cohosh is a large, many-stemmed herb springing from a thickened, creeping, perennial rootstock. The stems are 1 to 3 feet high, clasped near the base with 2 or 3 deformed sheathing leaves. Near the top of each stem is a single large 3-parted leaf, and at the stem's apex a cluster of compound leaves, each of the leaflets being several-lobed. Blossoms are small, star-shaped, bronzy-green, and in a loose group on stems springing from the uppermost leaves before the latter have fully developed. Blooms in late April and May and bears blueberry-like fruit about ⅓ inch in diameter. Found in deciduous woods and thickets—frequently on slopes—in humus-rich, acid or neutral soil (pH 4.5–7). Ranges from New Brunswick to Manitoba and south to S.C., Tenn., Neb., and Mo.

Easily cultivated and lends variety to the woodsgarden. Suffers little from pests or disease and requires a minimum of care. Propagation may be by seed or fall division of the rootstocks. A heavy wintercover of oak, beech, or mixed leaves should be left in place in the spring.

Bloodroot; Puccoon-Root (*Sanguina'ria canaden'sis*)

Bloodroot gets both its common and scientific names from the red juice of its creeping rootstocks, which often form a dense network just below the surface. The single leaves and flowers rise separately on long stems directly from the rootstocks; but at first the leaves completely enwrap the flower buds, which soon poke out at the top of the still-rolled leaves. Blossoms are white or pinkish, flat and starlike, rising to a height of 6 to 10 inches. Leaves, which are grayish-green, roundish, and deeply indented, eventually attain a height of as much as 12 to 14 inches and overtop the flowers.

Bloodroot blooms in late March or early April. It is an inhabitant of open woods with rich, neutral, or moderately acid soil, and is not infrequently found in partial shade along roadsides. Its range is wide—from N.S. to Man., and south to Fla., Ala., Ark., and Neb.

This is another excellent wildgarden plant, and requires little care if given rich soil of the right pH—about 6–7—partial shade and average moisture. Propagation is by root division or seed. A light wintercover of oak, beech, or mixed leaves is desirable and may be left in place.

Celandine-Poppy; Gold-Poppy (*Styloph'orum diphyl'lum*)
Superficially this yellow-flowered perennial resembles a buttercup, but its leaves are compound and its juice yellowish. The 12 to 14 inch stems rise from a thick rootstock; and the leaves are divided into several deeply toothed lobes, which are whitish beneath. Blossoms in the spring, and bears a rough, hairy, spindle-shaped dry fruit. Grows in deciduous woods in rich neutral or slightly acid soil, of pH 6–7. Scarce, or perhaps absent, in New England, but ranges from Pa. to Wis. and Mo.

This is a good woodsgarden plant, thriving under the conditions given above and requiring little care. However, there is a weed-like introduced European relative, with smaller flowers and smooth seed capsule, which must not be brought into the garden.

Sanguinaria canadensis   *Stylophorum diphyllum*

Mountain-Fringe; Alleghany Vine (*Adlu'mia fungo'sa*)
This is a slender, climbing biennial relative of the Dutchmans-breeches, growing to a height of several feet by clasping rocks and other plants with its leaf stems and by winding itself over and around its supports. The leaves are compound, and the leaflets delicate and 3-lobed. Flowers are tubular,

[111]

½ inch or more long, white, pink, or purplish, and hang in generous clusters among the leaves. Fruit is an oblong pod. Grows in cool, wet woods, on shaded ledges, and in thickets in moderately acid soil—about pH 5–6. Its range is from N.B. to Ont. to Wis. and south to S.C., Tenn., and Mich.

Mountain-fringe is an excellent wildgarden plant, not much subject to pests or disease, and often perpetuates itself by self-sown seeds. It is easily propagated by fall-planted seeds, the first year's growth being a striking rosette. The plant dies the second year, after ripening its seeds.

Adlumia fungosa

Dutchmans-Breeches (*Dicen'tra cuculla'ria*)

This is a close relative of the familiar garden bleedinghearts, and takes its common name from the pants-shaped blooms. The deeply cut, almost feathery leaves arise in a dense mass directly from the bulbous perennial base to a height up to 10 inches. The naked, somewhat fleshy flower stalk also springs from the rootstock, rises above the leaves, and bears 3 to 7 nodding, fragrant, double-spurred, white-and-yellow flowers. Blooms in April and May, and bears an oblong fruit pod, which splits lengthwise when the seeds have ripened.

Dutchmans-breeches are absent or rare near most of New England's coastline, but plentiful in the interior, especially in limestone regions. They typically inhabit rich deciduous, rather open woods and shaded rocky slopes and streambanks,

Dicentra cucullaria   *Dicentra canadensis*

sometimes growing in dense masses over considerable areas. Their preference is for humus-rich, slightly acid or neutral soil of pH 6–7, and they range from N.S. and Wis. to N.C., Mo., and Kan.

This is a favorite woodsgarden wildflower and does well under cultivation, except that it seldom blooms freely. Propagated by division of both crowns and roots.

Squirrel-Corn; Turkey-Corn (*Dicen'tra canaden'sis*)

Very closely resembles Dutchmans-breeches, but has more lacy, somewhat grayer leaves and blossoms without spurs. Fragrant with the odor of hyacinths. Name is derived from its numerous small bulb-like tubers. Habitat, range, and cultural requirements approximate those of *Dicen'tra cucul-la'ria*. Unfortunately the tubers are favorite mouse food.

Fringed Bleedingheart; Wild Bleedingheart
(*Dicen'tra exi'mia*)

This is a larger, coarser, pink-flowered perennial growing from heavy creeping rootstocks. Under ideal conditions the flower stalks may reach a height of 36 inches, and the plants may form a dense, rapidly spreading mass which, while itself highly pleasing, will smother most other herbs. It luxuriates in damp, rich, acid woods in a soil containing humus derived from pine needles and oak leaves. Optimum pH 4.5 to 5.5. Under such conditions our plants blossom from May to September, and are sometimes still blooming when cut down by frost. Not much bothered by pests or disease. Is a favorite in both wild and tame gardens, and increases rapidly by division and rootstock extension. Range from N.Y. to Ga. A white-flowered variety is widely sold by dealers.

Pale or Pink Corydalis (*Coryd'alis sempervi'rens*)

A delicate, lacy, 12 to 24 inch biennial which grows mostly in poor soil on gravelly slopes or in open rocky places, but

Dicentra eximia   *Corydalis sempervirens*

which sometimes thrives in open woods. Lower leaves are short-stemmed and from 1 to 5 inches long; upper ones smaller and sessile or nearly so; and both upper and lower compoundly divided into many-lobed leaflets. During its first summer the only foliage is a tight leaf-rosette flat on the ground; but in its second year the plant sends up many lacy, branched stems, tipped from May to September with loose bunches of spurred pink-and-yellow flowers which give place to clusters of relatively long and narrow seed pods. Grows in a wide variety of soils, ranging from moderately acid to slightly alkaline. Occurs from N.S. to Alaska, and south to Ga., Ky., Minn., and Mont.

Easily cultivated, and readily propagated by seed. Has maintained itself under our Pfitzer junipers for a dozen years or so. Thrives with us at pH 5–6. The roots of this and the following species have a strong odor when crushed.

Golden Corydalis (*Coryd'alis au'rea*)

Generally similar to its pink relative, but smaller and with yellow blossoms. Its habitat is open woodland, preferably in humus-rich, slightly acid or neutral soil (pH 6–7). Range about the same as that of *Corydalis sempervirens*. Other very closely similar species occupy parts of the same range.

A good woodsgarden plant, easily multiplied by seed.

Dentaria diphylla

Crinkleroot Toothwort, Crinkleroot, or Two-Leaved Toothwort (*Denta'ria diphyl'la*)

This little perennial has twin-stemmed, blackberry-like, dark-green leaves rising to a height of 6 to 14 inches from a notched, white rootstock which creeps through the surface humus of rich woods from N.S. and Ont. to Minn., and south to S.C. and Ky. The white or delicately pinkish blossoms cluster at the end of the stem above the two leaves. Blooms in late April and May. Seed pods are flattened and tapered. Prefers moderately acid soil (pH 5–6).

A nice woodsgarden plant. One appeared voluntarily in our garden about 8 years ago, and now we have several thriving clumps. Multiplies by rootstock division. Incidentally, this rootstock is exceedingly brittle, and each piece may generate a new plant. Light, leafy wintercover desirable.

Cutleaf Toothwort, or Pepper-Root (*Denta'ria lacinia'ta*)

Generally resembles the preceding species, except that there are usually 3 leaves to each stem, and the leaves are divided into deeply toothed narrow leaflets. Prefers open woods and slightly acid or neutral humus-rich loam of pH 6–7. Range: Que. to Minn., and south to Fla., La., and Kans.

Propagation similar to that of *Dentaria diphylla*.

Another plant, the large toothwort, has large pale-purple flowers and is rare and local.

Douglass or Lavender Bittercress (*Cardam'ine douglass'i*)

A delicate 6 to 12 inch plant from a tuberous perennial rootstock. Leaves are of 2 kinds—long-stemmed basal, and stemless toothed on the stalk. Purple flowers in a loose terminal group. Seed pods bean-like. Blooms April to May. Rich deciduous woods with nearly neutral (pH 6.5 to 7.5) soil. Northern N.A. A good plant for moist, shady spots. Propagated by seeds and division. Cultivation easy.

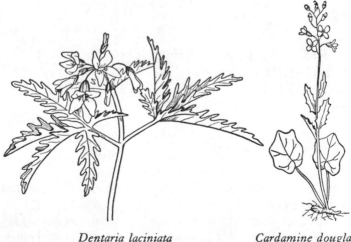

Dentaria laciniata   *Cardamine douglassi*

Foamflower; False Miterwort (*Tiarel'la cordifo'lia*)

Getting its name from its foam-like spikes of tiny white flowers, this little woodland plant spreads into large clumps by rooting its arched runners. Leaves rise on 4 to 8 inch stems directly from the stout underground perennial roots or from long surface runners, and are heartshaped, many-lobed, and pointed. The flower stalks also rise from the ground and may be up to 12 inches high. Blossoms appear from April to June. Grows best in rich, moist woods with from moderately acid to neutral soil (pH 5–7), but has done well in our garden at pH 4.5. Range: from N.S. and Ont. to Ga., Ind., Mich., and Minn.

A very attractive groundcover, easily multiplied by seeds or division of roots or rooted creepers. Must be kept moist and provided with rather dense shade. Snails and slugs are its worst enemies in our garden. A light oakleaf groundcover is desirable and may be left in place in spring.

Tiarella cordifolia   *Heuchera americana*

American Alumroot (*Heuche'ra america'na*)

A big brother to the foamflower and bishop's cap, the alumroot sends its leafless, hairy, sticky flower stalk to a height of from 18 to 36 inches and surrounds its upper third with loosely grouped, minute, greenish-bronzy and cup-shaped flowers. Leaves spring direct from the thick underground stem, and are fuzzy, oval, and several-lobed. Blooms from May to early August. Found in dry or rocky woods and on banks, from Ont., Ill., Mich., and Minn. south to Ga., and La.

Cultivation in all ways similar to that of foamflower. Likes well-drained humus-rich soil, of pH 5–6.

Miterwort, or Bishops-Cap (*Mitel'la diphyl'la*)

Closely related to the foamflower but more delicately graceful, this plant has basal, heartshaped, tooth-edged, hairy, stemmed leaves and a pair of similar but stemless leaves about two-thirds up the flower stalk. From the top leaves the small white flowers rise in a sparse spike 3 to 8 inches long, for a total height of about 10 to 18 inches. Blossoms in April and May. Inhabits rich, wet woods and streambanks from Que. to Minn., and south to N.C. and Mo.

Easy to cultivate, if you have a cool, shaded, wet spot, with a rich soil of pH 5–7—preferably about pH 6. Propagation by seed and root or runner division.

Mitella diphylla   *Gillenia trifoliata*

Bowman-Root (*Gille'nia trifolia'ta*)

Bowman-root is a member of the rose family, grows 2 to 4 feet high from a perennial root, and has several slender, branched stalks with many 3-parted stemless leaves and loose groups of slender-petaled white flowers at the upper extremities. Flowers in June and July. Inhabits rich, rather open woods and thickets, in moderately acid soil of pH 5–6; and ranges from Ont., N.Y., and Mich. south to Ga. and Mo.

Does well in a woodsgarden, and is propagated by seed and division.

Indian-Physic (*Gille'nia stipula'ta*)

Very similar to Bowman-root in appearance and cultural requirements, this plant reaches a height of 4 feet. Ont. to Ga., La., Ala., Mo., and Kans.

Barren Strawberry (*Waldstein'ia fragarioi'des*)

In general appearance this plant resembles a domestic strawberry, with stemmed, 3-parted, toothed leaves and branched flower stalks rising directly from a creeping rootstock. The yellow blossoms appear in May and June. Thrives in rocky woods, on shaded hillsides and banks, and on hummocks in swamps. Ranges from N.B. and Ont. to Ga., Ind., Mich., Minn., and Ore. Prefers humus-rich, moderately acid soil of pH 5–6.

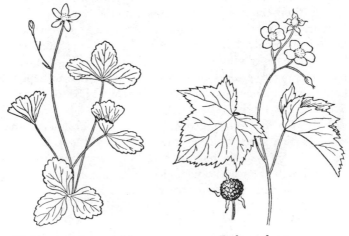

Waldsteinia fragarioides   *Rubus odoratus*

An interesting little plant which does well in cool woodsy spots, and does not appear to be bothered by disease or pests. Spreads by means of its creeping stems, and may occasionally need to be controlled. Common name from the fact that it bears no fleshy fruits.

[119]

Fragrant Thimbleberry (*Ru'bus odora'tus*)

This is a big, shrubby, branched, non-prickly, sticky-stemmed, raspberry-like plant from 3 to 5 feet high. The 3-to-5-lobed maple-like leaves are from 5 to 10 inches across and are somewhat hairy. The pink (occasionally white) flowers, up to 2 inches in diameter, are borne in loose clusters at the branch-ends. Fruit is raspberry-red, somewhat thimble-shaped, and insipid but edible. This unusual raspberry likes moderately or slightly acid soil (pH 5–6), in rocky deciduous woods and thickets and in cliff pockets. N.S. and Ont. south to Ga., Tenn., and Mich.

Thimbleberry is a striking plant for large woods or ledge-gardens, and is relatively immune to pests and diseases; but it spreads rapidly from deeply creeping underground stems and, once established, can prove a considerable nuisance.

Star-Violet; Dalibarda (*Dalibar'da re'pens*)

Although dalibarda is a close relative of the blackberries and raspberries, its general habit and appearance are violet-like and its long-stemmed white blossoms are reminiscent of the hepaticas. Leaves are long-stemmed; and are dark-green, downy on both sides, 1 to 2 inches in diameter, toothed, and blunt-heartshaped. Both leaves and flowers spring from perennial creeping rootstocks or stems. Blossoms June to September. Occurs in humus-rich, damp woods from N.S. to Minn., and South to N.C., Ohio, and Mich.

This is a fine groundcover plant for cool, moist, shaded woodsgarden spots with very acid soil of pH 4–5. It may also be grown in a shady bog garden. One very interesting thing about it is that in addition to its white star-shaped blooms, it bears numerous small self-fertilized flowers—like those of some violets—at or near the ground. Multiplies principally by spreading rootstocks.

Roadside Agrimony (*Agrimo'nia stria'ta*)

This is a tall herbaceous plant raising its stout, brownish-hairy, erectly branched stalk, topped with a spike of small yellow flowers, to a height of from 2 to 6 feet. Leaves and leaflets are numerous, alternate, divided, and toothed. Found in damp, open woods and thickets, and along roadsides, in moderately

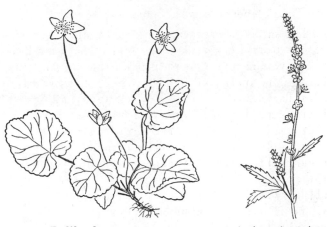

Dalibarda repens   *Agrimonia striata*

acid soil (pH 5–6), from Newfoundland to Saskatchewan, and south to W.Va., Neb., and Mex. Flowers from June to Sept.

Not a particularly desirable woodsgarden plant, but easy to grow. Propagated by seed or by division of the perennial rootstock. Usually not bothered by disease or pests; and indifferent to wintercover.

Woodland Flax (*Li'num virginia'num*)

An exceptionally graceful branched perennial herb with small, oval, stemless leaves and tiny, golden, star-like flowers interspersed with the leaves near the upper ends of the 12 to 24 inch stalks. Blooms June to July. Rocky woods and streambanks in northeastern, middle, and southern states.

A rather colorful plant for moist, cool, shaded spots with rich, slightly acid soil of pH 6–7. Propagated by seed, division, or softwood cuttings. No special care.

American Woodsorrel (*Oxa'lis monta'na*)

Woodsorrel is a superficially clover-like little plant with both leaves and blossoms rising on long stems directly from a slender, scaly, branched perennial rootstock. Leaves are from 2 to 6 inches high, fuzzy, 3-parted, and heart-shaped. Flowers are ½ to ¾ inch across, white or pinkish, with darker pink veins. A few specialized short-stemmed flowers are sometimes present

[121]

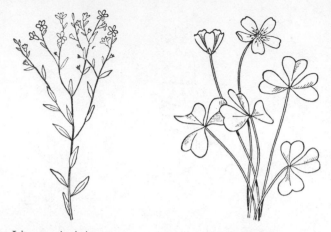

Linum virginianum   *Oxalis montana*

at the leaf bases. Fruit is a tiny pod about ⅙ inch long. Blossoms from May to July; is found in deep, cold woods or mossy banks in humus-rich acid soil (pH 4–5); and ranges from N.S. to Ont. & south to Ga. A very closely related species is found in Europe, Asia, and Africa.

Woodsorrel is a desirable groundcover, but can be grown only in shady, cool, damp locations.

Violet Woodsorrel (*Oxa'lis viola'cea*)

This is a tiny-leaved relative of the preceding plant, with groups of lavender-purple flowers on stalks rising high above the leaves—up to 8 inches tall. Blossoms in May and June; and is found in open dryish woods, thickets, and grasslands from Mass. to Minn. & south to Fla. and Tex. Rootstock is a brown, scaly bulb, from which the plants spread so rapidly by runners that they must be confined by a metal band or ruthlessly pulled up when out of bounds. Largely free from pests and disease. Prefers moderately rich, slightly acid soil of about pH 6.0 to 6.5.

Spotted or Wild Geranium; Cranesbill
(*Gera'nium maculd'tum*)

Wild geranium is about twice as large as herbrobert, rising as high as 20 inches from a stout perennial rootstock. Leaves are on long, hairy stems and are 3- to 6-parted, with deeply cut

Geranium maculatum

leaflets. Flowers are rose-purple, 1 to 1½ inches across. Fruit is an oblong capsule. Blossoms from late April to July; and ranges from Me., Ont. and Man. south to Ga. and La. Likes rich, open woods and damp, shaded roadsides in neutral or acid soil.

This geranium is a good woodsgarden denizen, for it seeds itself freely, does well under a great variety of conditions, and is pest- and disease-free. One plant, brought into our garden 18 years ago, has populated many semi-shaded spots all over our grounds. Acid tolerance is unusually wide, about pH 4.5 to 7.0.

Herbrobert Geranium (*Gera'nium robertia'num*)

Herbrobert is a true geranium, and is native not only to much of North America but to Europe and northern Africa as well. It is about 12 to 18 inches high, from an annual or biennial root, and may have one or several sticky-hairy stems. Leaves are 3-parted, with leaflets deeply toothed, and are attached by stems to nodes along the whole length of the main stalk. The tiny reddish-purple flowers appear near the stalk ends from May to September, and are followed by spindle-shaped seed capsules.

Inhabits rich, open woods and semi-shaded hillsides, usually in neutral or only slightly acid soil (pH 6–7). Range in North America from N.S. and Man. south to Pa. and Mo. Is easily grown in semi-shaded spots. Multiplies by seed, usually self-sown. Not often bothered by pests or diseases. Is sometimes called musk geranium because of its strong, disagreeable odor.

Fringed Polygala (*Polyg'ala pauci fo'lia*)

This tiny polygala, only from 3 to 7 inches high, is found in cool, rich, moist, deciduous woods; its rosy-purple (or rarely white) flowers conspicuous against the leafy groundcover, under which its long perennial stems creep freely, with occasional delicate roots penetrating downward into the humus. The stalks rise singly, or in small groups, and are tipped with one or several ¾ inch tubular flowers. Numerous closed, self-fertilized flowers occur on short subsurface stems. Large oval leaves clustered at stalk tops, around the flowers. Scale-like leaves below. Range: from New Brunswick to Saskatchewan and south to Ga., Ill., and Minn.

Fringed polygala is a lovely woodsgarden plant. Unfortunately, though, its long-creeping sparsely rooted stems make it very difficult to transplant; and it is subject to fungus diseases and slugs and other pests. Requires humus-rich soil of pH 4.5 to 5.0; and should be given a light oakleaf wintercover, preferably left in place in the spring. Propagation, while difficult, is possible by means of both seeds and stem cuttings.

Jerseytea; Redroot; New Jersey Tea
(*Ceano'thus america'nus*)

A low shrub, with many branches ascending from a deep, reddish, perennial root. The oval, hairy leaves, 1 to 3 inches long, are alternately disposed along the stalks. Flowers are tiny and white and are in dense long-stemmed clusters in the axils of the upper leaves. Blossoms in June and July. Occurs in sandy or dry, open woods and fields from Ont. and Man. to Fla. and Tex. A good plant for a large woodsgarden. Propagated by root division. Requires only moderately rich soil, of pH 6–7.

Giant St. Johnswort (*Hyper'icum as'cyron*)

A 3 to 6 foot herb, with clasping oval leaves and 1½-inch star-like yellow flowers at the apex of the branched stalk. Pear-shaped seed pods. Blooms in July. Moderately acid (pH 5–6) dry soil in open woods and thickets. Que. to Man. and south to Pa., Ill., Mo., and Kans. Fine for the large woodsgarden. No special care.

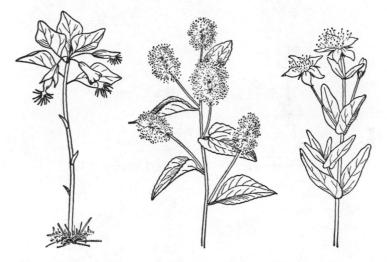

Polygala paucifolia   *Ceanothus americanus*   *Hypericum ascyron*

VIOLET FAMILY (*Viola'ceae*)

Violets are top favorites among wildflower enthusiasts, and several dozen species are grown in gardens of various kinds. Violets are hard for the novice to identify, for they differ only slightly one from another. But most members of this family are tolerant of cultivation, relatively pest- and disease-free, and reproduce themselves freely by seed or stem extension or both. A few spread through the wildgarden so rapidly that they must be considered as weeds. Those species listed below may be grown in a woodsgarden, under the conditions indicated for each; and we suggest that before any reader takes up a wild violet he first note carefully the circumstances under which it is growing.

Viola canadensis   *Viola conspersa*

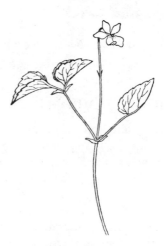

Viola emarginata .   *Viola ericarpa*

Viola incognita

Viola latiuscula

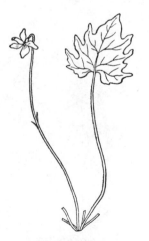

Viola palmata

Viola primufolia

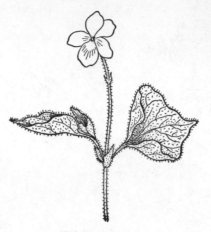

Viola pubescens

Viola rostrata

Viola rotundifolia

Viola selkerki

Viola septentrionalis

Viola sororia

Violet Names	Kind of Woods	Shade
Canada (white) (Viola canaden'sis)	open, moist, rich	medium
Amer. Dog (violet) (V. consper'sa)	moist, low, shaded	heavy
Triangle leaf (blue) (V. emargina'ta)	dry, open	light
Smooth (yellow) (V. ericar'pa)	open, moist, rich	light
Bigleaf (white) (V. incog'nita)	low, cool, moist	heavy
Beechwoods (violet) (V. latius'cula)	open, dry, sandy	light
Palmate (purple) (V. palma'ta)	dry, rich, open	light
Primrose (whitish) (V. primufo'lia)	moist, open, rich	light
Downy (yellow) (V. pubes'cens)	dry, rich	medium
Longspur (lilac) (V. rostra'ta)	cool, moist, rich	heavy
Roundleaf (yellow) (V. rotundifo'lia)	cool, moist, rich	heavy
Wilderness (violet) (V. selker'ki)	cool, moist, rich	heavy
Ontario (purple) (V. septentriona'lis)	moist, open	medium
Sister (lavender) (V. soro'ria)	moist, rich, rocky	medium

Readers wishing to identify the several species should consult one of

Common Meadow-Beauty; Deergrass (*Rhex'ia virgin'ica*)
More of a meadow than a woods plant, this 12 to 24 inch
succulent, square-stemmed, rather hairy plant is nevertheless
cultivatable in rich, very acid (pH 4–5) soil in a semi-shaded
part of the woodsgarden. Leaves are oval, toothed, and clasping. Flowers are bright purple or purplish-red, 1 to 1½ inches
across, and usually in near-terminal clusters. Blooms July to
Sept. Ranges from Me. and Ontario to Fla., La., Mo., and
Iowa.

Rhexia virginica   *Epilobium angustifolium*

pH	Bloom	Range
4–7	May to July	N.B. to Sask., & so. to S.C., & Ala., & Ariz.
5–6?	May & June	Que, to Minn., & so. to Ga.
6–7?	April & May	N.Y. to Ga. & west to Okla.
5–6?	May & June	N.S. to Man. & so. to Ga. & Tex.
5–6?	April & May	Que. to Wis., & so. to Mass. & Tenn.
6–7	?	Vt. to N.J. & n.w. Pa.
6–7?	April to June	Mass. to Minn., & so. to Fla.
5–6		N.B. to Fla. & La.
5–7		N.S. to N.D. & so. to Va. & Mo.
6–7?	May & June	Que. to Mich. & so. to Ga.
5–6?	May & June	Me. to Ont. & so. to Ga.
5–6?	April & May	Greenl'd & N.B. & so. to Ga.
6–7?	?	Newf. & B.C. and southward.
6–7?	April & May	Que. to Minn. & so. to N.C.

the several illustrated books on violets.

Fireweed (*Epilo'bium angustifo'lium*)

An eye-catching perennial herb, 3 to 8 feet high, with long, narrow, alternate, usually toothed leaves and a pointed spike of one-inch purple flowers. Blooms June to Aug. Fruit a bean-like pod, which snaps open to release the cotton-winged, wind-borne seeds. Derives its common name from the fact that although it is uncommon in established woods, it quickly invades burned-out northern forests to form dense masses of color sometimes visible for several miles. Ranges from Greenland to Alaska and south to N.C., Ind., Kan., and Calif. Can be grown in slightly acid (pH 6–7) soil of a woodsgarden, but is inclined to become weedy. No special care.

Wild Sarsaparilla (*Ara'lia nudicau'lis*)

A rather large, coarse herb often covering the forest floor almost to the exclusion of other vegetation. One leaf and one flower stalk rise directly from terminal points on the pencil-thick rootstock creeping just below the groundlitter. Leaves are divided into 3 separate leaflets, each of which is further divided into 5 toothed and pointed-oval leaflets. Flower stalk also 3-parted, somewhat shorter than leaf stalk, with terminal globe-shaped bunches of tiny white flowers which in the fall give rise to purplish-black berries. Rootstock sometimes used as

[131]

substitute for official sarsaparilla flavoring. Occurs in thin-soiled, mostly mixed or deciduous woods from Newfoundland westward and south to Ga., Colo., and Idaho. Apparently prefers moderately acid soil, of pH 5–6.

A legitimate occupant of good-sized woodsgardens, requiring no care at all and multiplying freely by rootstock extension. May become weedy—watch it!

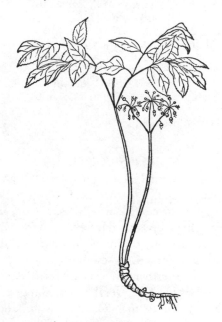

Aralia nudicaulis

Dwarf Ginseng; Groundnut (*Pan'ax trifo'lium*)

This small relative of the ginseng of commerce has a smooth stalk rising 3 to 6 inches from a globose (or round) perennial tuber, not more than ½ inch in diameter and having a decidedly pungent taste. There are three 5-parted, finely toothed leaves at the top of the stem. About 15 to 25 tiny white flowers are borne in a roundish tuft raised from 1 to 3 inches above the leaf stems. The fruit is a 2- or 3-lobed yellowish capsule. Grows in moist woods and thickets, in moderately acid to neutral soil (pH 5–7). Ranges from N.S. to Wisc., and south to Ga., and Iowa. Blooms from late April to early June.

[132]

This is a nice little woodsgarden plant, but must have quite moist, well-drained, humus-rich soil. It is not much bothered by disease or pests, and should be given winter protection, preferably of mixed leaves about 1 inch deep—which may be left in place in the spring. Propagation is by seed or division of the tubers.

Panax trifolium

American or True Ginseng (*Pan'ax quinquefo'lium*)

This is a much larger plant than the foregoing, and has a stalk rising 8 to 16 inches from a deep, often weirdly shaped perennial taproot. The leaflets are coarse and up to 4 inches long; flowers are greenish; and fruit 2-lobed, ½ inch across, and a brilliant red. Occurs in rich deciduous woods from Que. southward in the mountains to N.C. and Mo.

The root of a nearly related species occurring in Manchuria and Korea has been valued for centuries by the Chinese for its alleged ability to restore virility; and choicest cured roots, resembling a man in shape, have sold for fabulous prices—up to $400 an ounce. Because of the increasing scarcity of their own species the Chinese long ago turned to this American form, with the result that it has been both dug and cultivated here for scores of years and is now exterminated locally. Many books have been written on its cultivation.

Requires humus-rich soil, preferably of oak leafmold, of pH 4.5–6.

[133]

Harbinger-of-Spring; Pepper-and-Salt (*Erige'nia bulbo'sa*)

A very early-blooming small herb, with a single-leaved blossom stalk rising for a few inches from an onion-like tuber, and bearing 1 or 2 leaves each twice divided in 3 leaflets. Flowers white and dark red—hence 'pepper-and-salt.' Deciduous woods in rich, approximately neutral soil (pH 6.5 to 7.0), from Ontario to Minn. and southward. Interesting in the garden principally because of its very early blooming. No special care.

Erigenia bulbosa   *Cornus canadensis*

Bunchberry; Dwarf Cornel (*Cor'nus canaden'sis*)

In spite of its tiny size this is a blood brother of our big dogwood trees. Its slender 3 to 9 inch stalks rise from string-like perennial stems creeping through the leafmold just under the groundlitter. On the top of each stalk is a whorl of 3 to 9 (usually 6) stemless, oval, pointed leaves 1 to 4 inches long. Flower is compound on a short stem above the leaf-whorl, white with greenish or yellowish center. Fruit a cluster of bright-red berries at the very top of the stem. Blossoms May to July, depending on latitude, often forming dense white carpets on northern tundras and in wet spots in rich, open deciduous woods. Its range extends across Canada, and south to N.J., W.Va., Ind., Colo., and Calif. Occurs also in Asia.

[134]

This is a fine groundcover plant, but must have damp, cool, very acid, rich soil of about pH 4–5. In congenial surroundings its underground stems spread rapidly; and it can be propagated also by seed. Not much subject to disease, but needs protection from slugs.

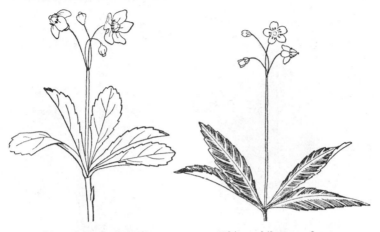

Chimaphila umbellata   *Chimaphila maculata*

Common Pipsissewa; Princespine (*Chima'phila umbella'ta*)

Pipsissewa is an evergreen little plant, with creeping semi-woody stems branching through the humus just below the groundlitter. From the underground stem arise erect branches bearing both leaves and flower stalks. The leaves are thick, shiny, practically stemless, bluntly oval, toothed, wider at the outer end, and cover the erect branch to a height of from 2 to 6 inches. The flower stalk rises straight up for 3 to 6 inches from the topmost leaves, and bears at its apex a cluster of small white or pinkish blossoms in July and August. Occurs in dry, open, rich woods (usually pine) in very acid soil (pH 4–5). Ranges across Canada and south to Ga. and Mex. Also in Eurasia.

A good woodsgarden groundcover plant, usually free from pests and disease. Propagation by division of the underground stems. An oakleaf winter cover is desirable, but should be removed in the spring.

[135]

Striped or Spotted Pipsissewa (*Chima'phila macula'ta*)

Very similar to the preceding species, but with narrower, deeply toothed, pointed leaves having white spots or stripes along the veins. Habitat, range, culture, and propagation like those of *Chima'phila umbella'ta.*

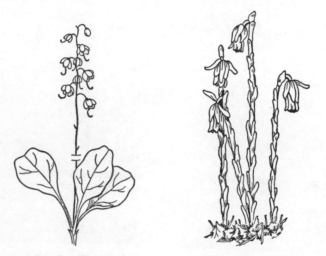

Pyrola elliptica   Monotropa uniflora

Waxflower Pyrola; Shinleaf (*Pyro'la ellip'tica*)

A common, if inconspicuous, little ground-hugging plant. Leaves from 1 to 5, thin, mottled brownish-green to dark green, oval or elliptical, rounded at their outer ends and narrowed near the base. Leaf stems about the same length as leaves, which arise in a bunch direct from the perennial roots. Flowers waxy-white, about ½ inch across, nodding on short stems, and arranged loosely around the upper part of an erect stalk springing from the leaf bases at the ground. Blooms June to August. Range N.S. to B.C. and south to Md., Ill., Iowa, and N.M. Occurs principally in rich, dry, coniferous or mixed woods and clearings, but sometimes thrives in wet thickets. Likes acid soil of about pH 4.5 to 5.5. Does well in a humus-rich woodsgarden. Reproduces by both seeds and runners; and is apparently not greatly bothered by pests or diseases.

[136]

American Pyrola; Roundleafed American Wintergreen
(*Pyro'la america'na*)

Somewhat like the preceding, but has smaller, oval, blunt, thick, shining, dark, evergreen leaves. Blossom stalk is 6 to 20 inches high, with the small pinkish-white flowers nodding from the upper one-third. Fruit a ¼-inch capsule. Blooms in June and July. Occurs in dry, usually sandy, acid soil—frequently under white pines. Range: N.S. west to N.D., and south to Ga., Ky., and Ohio.

A good woodsgarden plant, requiring soil of approximately pH 4.5 to 5.5.

Several other species of pyrola occur in the northern states.

Indian Pipe (*Monot'ropa uniflo'ra*)

A waxy-white or flesh-colored, scaly, succulent plant which usually grows in clusters from a tangle of brittle roots feeding on decaying plant matter. The stalks are 5 to 10 inches long, and the pipe-bowl-shaped flowers give the plant its name. Blossoms from June to August. When fruiting, the end of the flower stalk turns straight up. Inhabits moist, rich (usually deciduous) woods across North America and in Mexico, Japan, and the Himalayas. In New England does well in moderately acid soil of pH 5–6.

Almost impossible to transplant, because of the brittle root system entangled in decaying humus or other rotting plant matter. A very interesting plant, however, if you can get it and its food into your garden. Try lifting the plant, with a big shovelful of soil, when the ground is soaking wet, placing it immediately in a large flat box to give it support, and setting it gently into a woodscompost-lined hole in a moist, shady spot.

Pinesap (*Hypop'itys latisqua'ma*)

Very similar to the Indian pipe, but shorter and thicker, with color varying from buff to deep red. Flowers from July to September. Prefers rather dry pine woods. Ranges from Ont. and N.Y. to S.C. Optimum pH 4–5.

RHODODENDRONS, AZALEAS, LAURELS AND RHODORAS

All of these woody shrubs, some small and others almost tree-like, are closely related. Many are highly desirable for woods-gardens; all require humus-rich, acid soil; and all may be propagated in generally similar ways. For these reasons woods-gardeners anywhere may cultivate local species of all of these plants by merely modifying procedural details to approximate the conditions under which the plants grow wild.

Most importantly, members of this group must have extremely humus-rich, more or less acid soil. At least 50 percent of the soil should be composed of well-rotted acid plant material, which may include any or all of the following: woodsgarden compost, granulated peat, needlemold, leafmold of the strongly acid kinds, and various commercial organic materials. This soil should be brought to the needed acidity before it is used, and should be tested, and, if necessary, corrected at least annually thereafter. Aluminum sulphate, ammonium sulphate, and powdered sulfur are commonly used to acidify the soil. We prefer ammonium sulphate.

There should always be lots of groundlitter around shrubs of this group; and a heavy wintercover of oak or other strongly acid leaves or needles should be applied each fall and left in place the following spring. Different amounts of shade and water are required by the several species; but as a rule the plants thrive best if given light shade and frequent watering—though the soil must be well drained.

Very few members of this group can stand exposure to drying winds. Therefore they should be given windbreaks from fall to the time leaf or blossom buds begin to swell in the spring.

These shrubs should be transplanted in the very early spring, late summer or early fall. Some species have trailing underground branches, frequently not rooted, and are therefore difficult to handle. Often, however, young, or relatively compact, individuals can be found; and these may be readily transferred to your garden.

Amateur gardeners may best propagate members of this group by layerings or from seeds. Bark of layered branches should be cut at the buried areas; and layerings must not be separated from the parent plants for at least two years. Seeds should be treated with a disinfectant, sown in the fall or spring in equal parts of sterilized sharp sand and granulated peat, and very lightly covered with the same mixture. They must be kept constantly damp. The seedlings may, after they have at least 4 leaves, be transplanted into humus-filled flats or into special outdoor beds of the correct acidity. Young plants may be moved into the garden when two years old. Propagation may also be by cuttings of half-ripe wood; but the cuttings are very slow to root, and, in the amateur's hands, are more than likely to rot before taking hold.

RHODODENDRON GROUP

Common Name	Scientific Name	Shade	Moisture	pH
Pinxsterbloom A.	Aza'lea nudiflo'ra	Medium	Moist	4.5–6.0
Piedmont A.	Aza'lea canes'cens	Medium	Moist	4.5–6.0
Flame A.	Aza'lea lu'tea	Light or none	Moist	4.5–6.0
Rhodora	Rhodo'ra canaden'sis	Light or none	Wet	4.5–6.0
Rosebay	Rhododen'dron max'imum	Medium	Moist	4.5–6.0
Mountain Laurel	Kal'mia latifo'lia	Medium	Moist	4.5–6.0

Trailing Arbutus; Mayflower (*Epigae'a re'pens*)

This is an extensively creeping, semi-woody perennial, with alternate, leathery, broadly oval, evergreen leaves 1 to 4 inches long, and hairy at least on the growing stem tips. New leaves are often pinkish-brown. Flowers delightfully fragrant, white to pink, and clustered near the ends of the stems. Blooms in early spring. Fruit a hairy, fleshy, nearly globular capsule about ¼ inch in diameter. Seeds for propagation must be harvested soon after the capsule splits, for ants seek them out for food. Occurs in rich, sandy, or rocky woods in very acid soil, usually under pines or oaks. Range from Newf. to Sask. and south to Fla., Ky., and Wis.

Throughout its range the trailing arbutus is probably America's favorite wildflower. Unfortunately it is very sensitive to changed conditions, such as those brought about by lumbering and forest fires, and so has been exterminated from much of its former habitat. Moreover, it is practically impossible to pick arbutus flowers without seriously damaging the plant; and this, too, has helped to eliminate it from thickly populated areas. For these reasons several states have legislated strict protective laws—which should be conscientiously obeyed.

But trailing arbutus can be readily propagated from seed and from stem cuttings, and so can be legitimately sold by wild-flower dealers. Transplanting this plant from the wild is extremely difficult because of the long, sparsely rooted, trailing stems. However, isolated, stunted plants growing by themselves in unfavorable locations can be successfully brought into your garden and made to flourish there.

Favorable garden conditions include humus-rich, very acid soil of pH 4–5, a well-drained location preferably under pines or oaks, full shade, protection from slugs and rodents, and frequent light waterings. Wintercover of pine needles, partly removed in spring.

Scientific name means 'upon the earth'—from the little plant's prone habit.

Epigaea repens

Checkerberry Wintergreen; Spicy Wintergreen; Checkerberry (*Gaulthe'ria procum'bens*)

This little relative of the rhododendrons, azaleas, laurels, and trailing arbutus has semi-woody, extensively creeping underground stems from which the 2 to 6 inch branches rise erectly at irregular intervals. Leaves are 1 to 2 inches long, broadly oval, shallowly toothed, light-green below and darkly shiny evergreen above. The flowers are white or pinkish, ¼ to ½ inch long, bell-shaped, and hang on short stems under the leaves. Fruits are aromatic red berries, tasting of oil of wintergreen. Has an extremely variable habitat, ranging from full shade to bright sun, from clayey to sandy loam, from wet to very dry locations, and over a considerable range of acidity. Very common in most non-alkaline woods from Newf. to Man. and south to N.J., Ga., W.Va., Ind., and Mich.

An excellent groundcover throughout the more acid parts of your garden, at pH 4–6. Easy to grow, having few enemies; and readily propagated from stem cuttings and seeds. Birds and mice eat the berries.

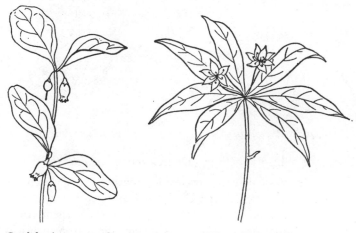

Gaultheria procumbens   *Trientalis borealis*

American Starflower (*Trienta'lis borea'lis*)

This wild relative of the primulas has a thread-like underground stem which creeps far and wide through leafmold just below the groundlitter and at intervals sends up single, slender stalks bearing a flat, wheel-like whorl of long, narrow, pointed leaves, and, above them, on very thin stems, one or more white star-shaped flowers wih golden centers. Blooms in May and June. Fruit a small spherical capsule. Moist, usually mixed coniferous and deciduous woods and thickets from Labrador and Man. south to Va., Mich., and Ill.

One of the most attractive groundcover plants for humus-rich, very acid (pH 4–5), shady spots. Spreads rapidly but is too delicate to crowd out other plants. Rather difficult to transplant, but easy to cultivate, for it has few enemies except aphids. Can be grown from seed or rootstock cuttings, but seldom needs to be.

Dodecatheon meadia   *Frasera carolinensis*

Common Shooting Star (*Dodeca'theon mea'dia*)

This is just one of many species of shooting stars, which occur in almost every part of the U.S. It is characterized by a rosette of basal leaves and a tall, smooth flower stalk rising from a heavy perennial rootstock. In this species the 4 to 6 inch leaves are narrowly oval, and the stalk about 1 foot high, topped by several rose-and-white, dart-shaped flowers—which look as if they were in a hurry to go somewhere, and give the plant its name. Other species and varieties have differently shaped leaves and flowers of various colors. Habitats of the shooting stars vary greatly; but this one is found in grasslands, open woods, and on cliffs and slopes, usually in moderately rich acid soil. Blooms in late spring. Ranges from Man. to Pa. and Tex.

Many species and varieties of shooting star are cultivated and are excellent for suitable spots in the woodsgarden. This species does best in only semi-shade and well-drained, not-too-rich soil of pH 4.5–6. Propagation is by division and seeds. Not particularly bothered by pests. Light wintercover.

Caroline Frasera; Columbo; Monument-Plant
(*Fra'sera carolinen'sis*)

A very large member of the gentian family, increasing by seed and dying in its third year (i.e. a 'triennial'). During the first and second years there is no flower stalk; only a rosette of long, narrow leaves broadest at their outer ends. In the third year the heavy stalk grows to a height of from 3 to 7 feet, bearing whorls of lily-like leaves and, on its terminal 6 to 12 inches, groups of short-stemmed, yellow-green-brown-and-purple flowers 1 inch across. Summer-blooming. Mich. to Ga. and Mo.

Can be transplanted into a semi-shaded woodsgarden with dryish, slightly acid soil of pH 6–7. Light groundcover desirable, but not necessary.

Virginia Pennyleaf (*Obola'ria virgi'nica*)

A small perennial plant nourished by decaying plant matter and having a brown-scaled, leafless stalk bearing branched clusters of small lilac-white flowers. Common name derived from the shape and color of the stalk scales. Blooms in spring. Humus-rich woods, in middle and southern states. An interesting garden plant, requiring pure leafmold of pH 5–6. Very difficult to transplant. Leafy wintercover, left on in spring.

Spreading Dogbane (*Apoc'ynum androsaemifo'lium*)

This 2 to 5 foot perennial has milky juice, opposite oval leaves 2 inches to 4 inches long, and small groups of tiny pink flowers near the branch tips. Blooms in summer. Open woods and thickets in moderately acid, rich soil of pH 5–6. Spreads so rapidly from creeping underground stems that it seldom should be placed in a garden.

[143]

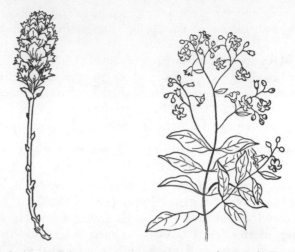

Obolaria virginica   *Apocynum androsaemifolium*

Sweet-William Phlox; Wild Blue Phlox (*Phlox' divarica'ta*)

This native perennial phlox is widely cultivated, and many varieties have been developed. Typically it is a semi-procumbent plant, the stems rooting at the joints and only the branch ends standing erect for a height of 12 to 24 inches. Leaves opposite and oblong. Flowers violet-blue to mauve clustered at stalk ends. Blooms May to June. Seeds in capsules. Rich, open woods from Que. to Fla. and Tex. Easily cultivated in lightly shaded, humus-rich soil of pH 6–7. Propagated by seed, division, and rooted stems. Relatively pest-free. May become weedy.

Creeping Polemonium; Greek Valerian
(*Polemo'nium rep'tans*)

Although this is a member of the phlox family, it superficially resembles a wild pea. The weak, slender stalk, with compound, alternate, somewhat fern-like leaves, rises from a branched perennial root and is topped by loose groups of light-blue or violet, bell-shaped flowers about ¾ inch long. Blooms April to May. Open woods and thickets, with slightly acid or neutral soil of pH 6–7. N.Y. to Ala. and Kans.

A desirable wildgarden plant, requiring little care. Propagated by seed and rootstock division. Indifferent to wintercover.

[144]

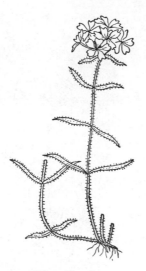

Phlox divaricata   *Polemonium reptans*

Virginia Waterleaf (*Hydrophyl'lum virginia'num*)
One of several species of waterleaf found, collectively, over most of southern Canada and northern U.S. This one is a 12 to 24 inch perennial herb with a slender branched stalk, alternate compound toothed leaves, and loose, terminal clumps of purple bell-shaped flowers ⅓ inch long. Blooms in May and June. Fruit a capsule. Open woods, in slightly acid or neutral rich soil of pH 6–7, from Que. to S.D. and south to S.C., and Kans. *Hydrophyllum appendiculatum* is somewhat similar, but likes neutral soil (about pH 7) and occurs in the northeastern U.S. It is a biennial.

Virginia waterleaf is easily cultivated and requires very little care. Propagated by seed and division. Light wintercover of mixed leaves.

Pursh Phacelia; Miami Mist (*Phace'lia pursh'i*)
An 8 to 15 inch annual with hairy, branched stem, deeply cut alternate leaves, and several small, flat, white-centered purple flowers at the stalk apex. Blooms in spring. Open, moist woods and fields in neutral (about pH 7) soil, Pa. to Minn. and south. A good garden plant. Cultivation easy. Light, leafy wintercover. Propagated from spring-sown seed. Common name

[145]

from Miami Valley, Ohio, where it sometimes carpets the ground with its misty-purple flowers.

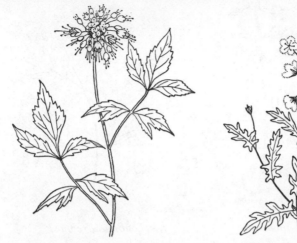

Hydrophyllum virginianum   *Phacelia purshi*

Virginia Bluebells; Virginia Cowslip
(*Merten'sia virgin'ica*)

Erect 12 to 24 inch branched stems from a perennial rootstock. Leaves gray-green, stemless or nearly so, oval, 2 to 5 inches long. Purple-pink-and-blue flowers shaped like long, slender bells and clustered at the branch-ends. Blossoms in April and May. In damp, open woods, in meadows and on stream banks from Ont. to Minn., and south to S.C. and Kans. Likes rich, nearly neutral soil of pH 6–7.

One of the most desirable plants for a damp, semi-shaded spot. Propagated by both seed and division. Relatively pest-free. Light maple-leaf wintercover. Foliage disappears after flowers fade, so that plant location must be marked. Best transplanted just as foliage dies.

Oswego Beebalm; Scarlet Bergamot (*Monar'da did'yma*)

Although more often found in the open than in forests, this 2 to 4 foot perennial is a justifiable denison of the woodsgarden. It is sparingly branched; has large, pointed-oval, toothed, usually hairy, dark-green leaves; and flaming-red, terminal, bunched flowers about 1½ to 2 inches long. Blooms in July and

[146]

Mertensia virginica   *Monarda didyma*

Aug. Moist soil, especially along streams but sometimes in open woods, from Que. to Ont., and south to Ga., Tenn., and Mich.

A colorful garden plant at a time when most woodsgardens are apt to be rather drab. Likes rich, somewhat acid soil of pH 5.5 to 6.5, only light shade, and lots of water. Easy to cultivate, having few pests and diseases. Propagated by division and from seed. Wintercover optional.

Citronella Horsebalm; Stoneroot (*Collinso'nia canaden'sis*)

A large, coarse perennial, up to 5 feet tall, with large, oval, toothed leaves to the top of the stalk, and long, branched terminal spikes of tiny golden-yellow flowers with a distinct lemony odor. Blooms Aug. to Sept. Moist, rocky woods in humus-rich, slightly acid or neutral soil (pH 6–7) from Que. to Wis., south to Fla., Ala., and Ark. Readily cultivated. Wintercover. Pest-free.

Blue-Eyed-Mary (*Collin'sia ver'na*)

A pretty annual, 8 to 24 inches high, branched, and bearing groups of stemmed blue-and-white flowers springing from the bases of the clasping, toothed, pointed, opposite leaves. Blooms in April and May. Moist open woods from N.Y. to Wisc. and Ky., in rich, slightly acid or neutral soil of pH 6–7. Grown in the woodsgarden from seed planted as soon as ripe—about

[147]

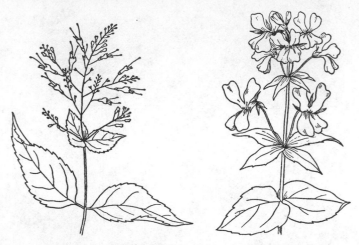

Collinsonia canadensis   *Collinsia verna*

midsummer. Usually develops a leaf-rosette in the fall and blooms early the next spring. Likes a medium-heavy winter-cover and must be protected from slugs and snails.

Early Pedicularis; Wood-Betony (*Pedicula'ris canaden'sis*)

A perennial plant having a feather-like mass of much-divided leaves and flower stalks rising 6 to 18 inches, all hairy. Yellowish or reddish-brown flowers—there's a lot of color variation—in short, broad, terminal clusters. Blooms from late April to June. Fruit a flattened oblong capsule. Open, dry woods and damp grasslands, in soil of pH 5.5 to 7.0, from N.S. to Man., and south to Fla., Kans., and Colo.

An interesting woodsgarden plant, difficult to transplant successfully because the roots of some individuals are at least partly attached to, and parasitic on, the roots of surrounding plants. Propagated by seed and division. Needs protection from slugs and snails. Rabbits love it!

Oakleech (*Aureola'ria pedicula'ria*)

A 2 to 4 foot perennial, obtaining part of its nourishment from oak roots. Leaves opposite, compound, and somewhat fern-like. Yellow blossoms near stem-ends about 1½ inches long and trumpet-shaped. Blooms June to Aug. Fruit a capsule.

Perdicularis canadensis   *Aureolaria pedicularia*

Plant covered with sticky hairs. Open woods, in rich acid soil of pH 4.5 to 5.5. Almost impossible to transplant, because its roots are attached to those of its 'host'; but can be grown from seeds planted over living oak roots. Likes oakleaf winter-cover. Not much bothered by pests or disease. Interesting principally because of its parasitic habit. Range: Me. to Ont. and Minn., and south to Fla. and Mo. There are several related species, notably *Aureolaria glauca*.

Beechdrops (*Epifa'gus virginia'na*)

A parasitic plant with no green coloring matter at all, getting its nourishment from the roots of beech trees. Consists of a cluster of much-branched stalks, 6 to 20 inches tall, brownish- or purplish-yellow, rising from brittle, fibrous roots. Yellow flowers are scattered along the stalks, upper blossoms ½ inch long and tubular and lower ones much smaller. Blooms Aug. to Oct. Fruits ¼ inch capsules, mostly from lower flowers. Dead stalks often remain upright through winter. Beech woods, N.S. to Ont. and south to Fla., La., and Mo.

An interesting woodsgarden plant, not transplantable, but sometimes introduced by seeds sown under beech trees. No special care. Humus-rich soil of pH 4.5 to 6.0. Oak or beech leaf wintercover.

Epifagus virginiana   *Conopholis americana*

Squawroot (*Conoph'olis america'na*)

A mass of fleshy underground stems from which thick scaly flower stalks, lacking in green matter, ascend to a height of 3 to 10 inches and bear near their tops many small yellow flowers partly hidden by scales. Blooms in May and June. Fruit an oval capsule. Rich, usually oak or beech, woods in moderately acid soil (pH 4–6), from Me. to Ont. and Mich., and south to Fla., Ala., and Tenn. Obtains its nourishment from roots of near-by trees. Very interesting in the garden, but must be established by planting seeds near living tree roots—preferably those of oaks.

Ghostpipe; Cancer-Root; Broomrape (*Thales'ia uniflo'ra*)

This is a strange, almost colorless plant, with many single-flowered, leafless stalks rising 3 to 8 inches from a tangled mass of underground stems which absorb nourishment from the roots of any one of several herbs. Flowers are pipe- or trumpet-shaped and a pale-lavender color. Blooms from May to June. Fruit a small oval capsule. Humus-rich, moderately acid soil (pH 5–6) in woods and thickets from Newf. to Ont., and south to S.C. and Tex.

[150]

An exceedingly interesting woodsgarden plant, but very
difficult to introduce. Try both seed and transplanting the roots
along with their 'host'—and just possibly you may succeed.

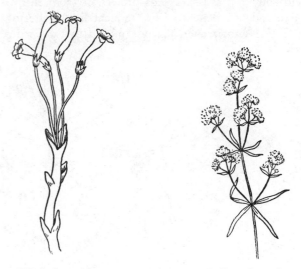

Thalesia uniflora   *Galium boreale*

Northern Bedstraw (*Ga'lium borea'le*)

One of a numerous group that covers much of northern North
America, Europe, and Asia. This species is 12 to 24 inches
high and many-branched, has long narrow leaves in whorls
of four, and is topped by a filmy mass of tiny white flowers.
Fruit a small, hairy capsule. Blooms May to Aug. Along
streams and in open, rocky, moist woods in somewhat acid
(pH 5–7), rich soil, from Que. to Alaska, and south to Pa.,
Mich., Mo., N.M. and Calif. Name derived from use as
mattress stuffing. Suitable for wildgarden, requiring no special
care. Propagated by division of perennial roots and from seeds.

Partridgeberry; Twinberry; Squawberry
(*Mitchel'la re'pens*)

An evergreen creeper, with rooted surface stems, small roundish evergreen leaves, and twin, pinkish, tubular, fragrant flowers developing into red berries having a mildly pepperminty
flavor. Blooms April to June. In needle and leaf mold of pine,

hemlock, and mixed woods, from N.S. and Ont. south to Fla., Minn., Ark., and Tex.

Should be in every woodsgarden, in full or partial shade and acid soil of pH 4–5. Needs protection from slugs, snails, birds, and rodents. Benefitted by frequent light waterings, and needle or leaf wintercover, partly removed in the spring.

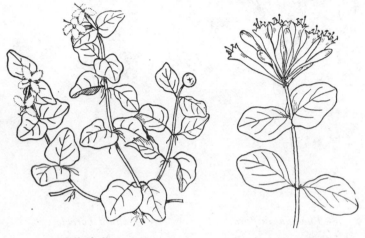

Mitchella repens   *Lonicera sempervirens*

Trumpet or Coral Honeysuckle (*Loni'cera sempervi'rens*)

Probably the brightest-flowered wild honeysuckle. A high-climbing vine, with dark-green, paired, oval, opposite leaves. Flowers scarlet-and-orange, long-trumpet-shaped, and clustered at branch-ends. Blooms July to Aug. Fruit, scarlet berries. Rich, acid soil (pH 5–6) in moist, cool woods from Newf. to B.C. and south to Md., Colo., and Calif.

A grand garden plant under appropriate circumstances. Relatively pest-free. Propagated by seeds, layerings, or softwood cuttings. Leafy wintercover.

Twinflower; Deervine (*Linnae'a borea'lis*)

A long-trailing, evergreen, vine-like member of the honeysuckle family, with small, opposite, roundish leaves. Flowers pink or white, bell-shaped, fragrant, and in pairs on slender 4 to 6 inch stems. Fruit a globular capsule containing only one seed. Humus-rich, very acid (pH 4–5) soil in cold, wet woods and swamps, and on shaded banks. Across N.A. and south to Md., Minn., Colo., and Calif.

A delightful woodsgarden plant needing little protection. Propagated by seeds and rooted stem cuttings. Oakleaf wintercover, partly removed in spring.

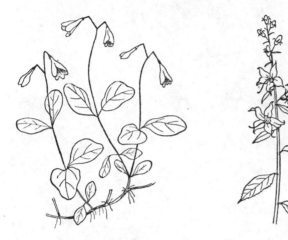

Linnaea borealis   *Campanula americana*

American Bluebell (*Campan'ula america'na*)

A tall plant, with a straight, leafy, flower-topped stalk up to 6 feet high. Leaves sharply oval, toothed and alternate. Flowers violet-blue, star-shaped, 1 inch across, and spring from the leaf-axils. Annual or biennial. Blooms June to Aug. Slightly acid or neutral soil (pH 6–7), in shady spots of rocky woods through much of eastern North America. Can be grown from seed. No special care. Wintercover immaterial.

White Snakeroot (*Eupato'rium rugo'sum*)

An erect, much-branched perennial up to 4 feet tall. Leaves opposite, pointed-oval, toothed, 3 to 6 inches long and 1 to 3 inches wide. Flowers tiny, white, on branched stems near top of stalk. Blooms Aug. to Oct. Rich, slightly acid or neutral soil of pH 6–7, in open woods, thickets, and clearings, N.B. to Ont., and south to Fla., La., and Neb. Interesting for large

[153]

woodsgardens, spreading rapidly by seed. May become 'weedy.'
No special care. Wintercover immaterial.

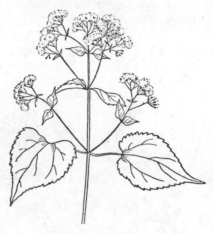

Eupatorium rugosum

GOLDENRODS

This is a numerous tribe over most of N.A., and many species
are suitable for cultivation in an appropriate type of wildgarden. Only a relatively small number, however, are woods
plants; and of these all are perennials, and multiply by both
seed and root division. Goldenrods are desirable in a woodsgarden because they bloom in late summer and autumn, but
there is some danger that they will become 'weedy.' None
require special care, except perhaps some protection against
insects (especially aphids) and blight. Wintercover is desirable, but usually not needed. Most types thrive in acid, humus-
rich soil of pH 5–6.

The best procedure with this group—all of which are very
easily transplanted in the early summer or late fall—is to
decide on the plants you want, study the conditions under
which they are growing, and then give them the same tpye
of soil, shade, etc. from which you take them.

Common Name	Scientific Name	Range
Silver Goldenrod	Solida'go bi'color	P.E.I. & Ont. to Ga., Tenn., & Minn.
Plume Goldenrod	Solida'go jun'cea	N.B. to N.C. & Mo.
Fragrant Goldenrod	Solida'go odo'ra	N.S. to Fla. & Tex.
Noble Goldenrod	Solida'go specio'sa	Mass. to N.C. & Ark.
Wreath Goldenrod	Solida'go cae'sia	N.S. & Minn. to Fla. & Tex.
Zigzag Goldenrod	Solida'go flexicau'lis	N.S. & N.B. to Ga., Tenn., & Mo.

Aster acuminatus   *Aster divaricatus*

Acuminate or Mountain Aster (*As'ter acumina'tus*)

Stems to 3 feet tall, with pointed-oval, sharply toothed, fuzzy leaves. Flowers 1 to 1½ inches broad, whitish or light purple, gold centers, rather droopy appearance. Blooms July to Oct. Moist woods and thickets, Labrador to Ontario and south to Ga. and Tenn. Good garden plant. pH 5–6. Little care. Wintercover. Multiplied by root division.

White Wood Aster (*As'ter divarica'tus*)

Slender-stalked plant 1 to 2 feet high. Lower leaves stemmed and almost heart-shaped. Upper ones unstemmed. Flowers 1

[155]

inch across, white, ragged, and golden- or bronzy-centered. Blooms July to Oct. Open woods, in soil of pH 5–7, Que. to Ga. and Tenn. Not a very good garden plant, for it is likely to spread too rapidly.

Aster lateriflorus   *Aster umbellatus*

Calico Aster (*As'ter lateriflo'rus*)

Grows to 5 feet from a perennial rootstock. Lower leaves oval and toothed and upper ones narrowly oblong. Stem branched. Flowers 1 inch across, whitish or pale purple, with gold centers. Blooms Aug. to Oct. Open woods, thickets, and fields, N.S. to Ont., and south to N.C., La., and Tex. Good woodsgarden plant. No special care. Propagated by division and seed. Wintercover desirable. Soil, pH 4–6.

Flat-top Aster (*As'ter umbella'tus*)

Rigid, erect stems, much-branched near top, to 8 feet high. Leaves stemless or nearly so, long and narrow, fuzzy beneath, and with slightly hairy edges. Flowers small and ragged, clustered at branch-ends, white with golden or pinkish centers. Blooms July to Oct. Moist, open woods, thickets, and fields, Newf. to Sask., and south to Ga., Mich., and Iowa. Good garden plant. pH 5–6. Little care. Wintercover. Multiplied by root division.

[156]

Cutleaf Coneflower (*Rudbeck'ia lacinia'ta*)

A sunflower-like perennial up to 10 feet high, with branched, leafy stalk. Leaves thin, hairy above and on edges, long-stemmed and divided into 5 or more leaflets on lower stalk and less divided and stemless near top. Stemmed flowers at apex of stalk, 3 to 4 inches across, with cone-shaped, greenish-yellow centers and back-tilted golden rays. Center cones elongate and become brownish as seeds ripen. Blooms July to Sept. Moist thickets and woods in slightly or moderately acid soil (pH 5–7), from Que. to Man. and south to Fla., Ariz., and Idaho.

The familiar domestic 'golden glow' was developed from this plant. Spreads by underground stems and must usually be controlled. Good for the large woodsgarden, requiring little care and furnishing welcome summer color.

Rudbeckia laciniata   *Helianthus divaricatus*

Divaricate, or Woodland Sunflower
(*Helian'thus divarica'tus*)

Up to 7 feet tall, this slender sunflower has long, narrow, stemless, opposite leaves, rough on their upper sides. Flowers are about 1 to 2 inches across, gold with bronzy centers. Blooms July to Sept. Dry woods and thickets, Ont. to Man. and south to Fla., La., and Neb. Lends late-summer color to the large woodsgarden, but may spread too rapidly. Pest-free. Wintercover desirable. Acceptable pH 5–7.

[157]

FERNS

Ferns are an extraordinarily ancient type of plants. Together, giant dinosaurs and towering tree-ferns dominated animal and plant life scores of millions of years ago—long before the pines, hardwoods, or flowering plants had appeared on earth. Yet today's ferns, decadent representatives of a glorious past, number more than 6,000 species and populate every continent. They are among our most interesting woods plants, and most certainly should be prominent in every woodsgarden.

Ferns literally lead a double life; for those you see in woods and meadows, along roadsides and streams, in rock crevices and on cliffs are only the asexual, spore-bearing generation. Each fern, in the form in which you know it, has sprung not from a seed but from a tiny, green, scale-like, sexual plant no bigger than your little fingernail and totally unknown to anyone but the skilled botanist.

The asexual generation of ferns does not bear seeds, but instead develops spores in special 'fruit dots' or spore cases usually located on the underside of the leaves, or fronds. These spores are dust-fine and are the dormant phase in the fern life cycle. They may remain alive for long periods under the most adverse conditions of temperature and drouth. For instance, spores of an Asiatic species have been recovered from the air high above one of our southwestern deserts, having been borne half around the earth by the ever-frigid currents of the near-stratosphere.

But when a fern spore does happen upon just the right conditions of temperature, humidity, shade, and soil—perhaps in a rock crevice, on the humus under a leaf, in the rough bark on the north side of a live oak, or even on bare earth or stone in the moist shade of a wall—a marvelous transformation takes place. The dry spore cracks open and from it there ooze cells, which quickly multiply to produce a prothalium—the sexual form of the plant—tiny, flat, rooted on its underside, and green above. Soon, on the moist lower surface of the prothalium, there appear specialized areas which in time give rise to eggs and spermatozoa. An infinitesimal percentage of the latter, by means of their pollywog-like tails, wiggle their way toward, and finally into, the eggs. In about 2 to 6 months after fertilization, small, primitive, green fronds appear, and within

[158]

a year or two the young plant becomes the asexual fern with which you are familiar.

Ferns, like wildflowers, may be propagated in several ways— by division, cuttings, and layerings. They may also be grown from spores, by the following procedure.

Pick the spore-bearing fronds, or parts of fronds, as soon as the ripening spores will darken a white surface rubbed against them, and place the fronds in an envelope or paper bag till the spores are needed for planting. Then prepare seed pots as suggested in Chapter viii of Part i, except that the soil in the upper part of the pot should consist of equal parts of finely sifted leafmold and sand. The top of the soil should then be pressed perfectly flat, and the lower part of the pot immersed in water of appropriate reaction (pH). Next, dust spores onto the surface of the dampened soil, and cover the pot with glass or cellophane to maintain a humid atmosphere above the soil. Place no sand or soil over the spores—they must lie on the surface—and water the pot only from below, preferably with water that has been sterilized by boiling. Keep pots well shaded, either outdoors or in, depending on the time of year.

'Grandmother'—not ours, maybe yours—is said to have grown ferns by simply spreading spores over a very thin coating of sifted leafmold on a brick kept standing in a pan of water. Why not try it?

In any event, after the young ferns have produced several fronds and are reasonably well rooted, transplant them to small individual pots filled with the half-and-half mixture of leafmold and sand. Set pots on a half-inch layer of sand in a shallow box having plenty of drainage holes, and fill the spaces between the pots with leafmold or pulverized peat. Keep this box in the shade, indoors or out, and keep the soil damp with a rose-spray or child's watering pot.

Our hardy northern ferns require about the same humus-rich soil, and respond to the same cultural practices, as do their wildflower associates. They multiply rapidly, are long-lived, and are little bothered by pests or diseases. But, except as noted in the following text, ferns must have shade, plenty of ground moisture, and protection from drying winds. On the whole, however, they are as easy to grow as they are ornamental. Leafy wintercover is desirable, and may be left in place in the spring,

[159]

for the young fronds will easily force their way up through it. The beginner at woodsgardening may expect considerable initial difficulty in identifying ferns—just as we, the authors, have found it almost (perhaps quite) beyond our power to describe the several species adequately in lay terms. Moreover, certain groups of ferns (notably the 'woodferns') show such great variation among the plants of a single species that even authorities disagree on both nomenclature and the identification of individual plants.

But careful study of this text and of some good fern book, along with close observation of wild ferns at various seasons of the year, will make you a fern 'expert' (at least in the opinion of your even-more ignorant friends) surprisingly soon. So don't be dismayed—just get started.

Common Polypody, Rock-Cap Fern
(*Polypo'dium vulga're*)

A small, evergreen fern usually found in dense, carpet-like masses on boulders, ledges, and very rocky slopes. It prefers moist, shaded locations on north or northeast exposures. Fronds are from about 4 to 12 inches long, once pinnate, with large, round fruit dots without covers. Below the frond masses are tangles of scaly brown rootstocks often woven into mats that can be rolled up like carpets. It is these underground stems that give polypodies their common and scientific names, for polypodium means 'many feet.'

Although, as might be expected from so wide-ranging a species, this fern will thrive in soil of various degrees of acidity, it commonly flourishes on granite boulders and ledges where the soil is pH 4–6. Polypodies, of this and very closely related species or forms, range from Newf. to Alaska and south to Ala., Ark., and Ga.

A southern relative, the Resurrection fern (*P. polypodioi'des*), is found on hummocks at bases of trees, on mossy cliffs, on tree trunks, and even on the tops of branches many yards up in the air—being especially partial to ancient, moss-draped oaks of various kinds where the moist bark among the polypody roots tests pH 3.75 to 4.5. It ranges over tropical America northward to Iowa and the central Atlantic states. The name of this species is derived from its habit, during dry weather, of curling up with the brown, hairy undersides of the fronds outward, and then almost miraculously becoming erect and green with the first heavy rain.

It is said that in ancient times an infusion of polypody fronds and rootstocks was used to drive away 'fearsome dreams and nightmares.'

Polypodies can easily be established on any suitable ledge, rock, or tree base in your woodsgarden. In fact they will sometimes grow readily—though rather incongruously—as a groundcover under pines and rhododendrons. They must be given plenty of moisture, and protection from bright sun and drying winds. No other special care is required. We have found it advantageous to work half an inch of oak leafmold or woodsgarden compost (pH 4.5 to 5.5) among the frond masses each fall. Propagation is so easy by division and root-stock cuttings that growing from spores is usually not worthwhile.

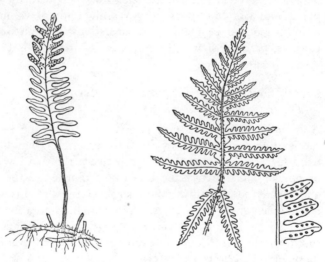

Polypodium vulgare   Dryopteris phegopteris

Narrow Beechfern (*Dryop'teris phegop'teris*)

A small, graceful, rather light-green fern with far-creeping, much-branched rootstocks by means of which it sometimes forms dense masses of beautiful groundcover and again spreads

[161]

itself rather sparsely among the surface rocks and rotting logs of damp hardwood or mixed forests with rich, definitely acid soil. Fronds are from 6 to 18 inches tall, broadly oval in outline; twice-pinnate, with brown scales on the stem, and hairy throughout. The lowest pair of pinnae are as long or longer than the rest and point downward and forward; and the stem between them and the next pair is bare except for tiny scales. The upper pinnae are not divided quite to the stem, and the end of the frond tapers quickly to a spear-like point. Fruit dots have no covers, are small and round, and are near the edges of the pinnules. This species is found in northern lands around the world; and in North America extends from Newf. to Alaska and south to Ga., Tenn., Iowa, and Wash.

The beechfern thrives in shady, moist locations where its rootstocks can easily creep through a deep layer of leafmold just below the groundlitter. It is also partial to dripping-wet ledges, and crevices with plenty of rich soil. Although tolerant of widely different soil acidities, it grows best with us at about pH 4.0 to 5.0. Multiplies very rapidly under favorable conditions, and can be readily propagated by division, rootstock cuttings, or from spores. In our woodsgardens it is pest- and disease-free.

Broad, Southern, or Winged Beechfern
(*Dryop'teris hexagonop'tera*)

A grand woodsgarden fern, closely resembling the preceding species but recognizable by its broader, more triangular outline, the lack of a bare stem-area between the two lower pairs of pinnae, and the fact the lowermost pinnae are the longest and usually point neither downward nor forward. Fronds may reach a length of 24 inches. Prefers rich, moist, moderately acid (pH 5–6) hardwood forests. Ranges from Que. and Minn. south to the Gulf States. Propagation and cultivation like those of the narrow beechfern.

Oakfern (*Dryop'teris disjunc'ta*)

An exceedingly graceful little fern, superficially resembling the familiar but larger bracken. Oakfern fronds—only from about 8 to 16 inches tall—are twice-pinnate, with the lowermost pair of pinnae so long as to suggest branches. New fronds

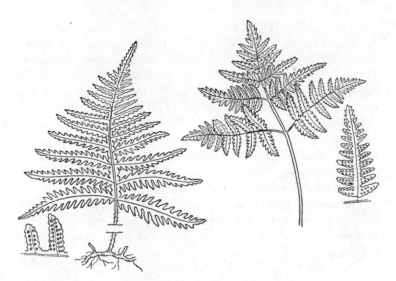

Dryopteris hexagonoptera   *Dryopteris disjuncta*

are formed throughout the summer, and when uncoiling exhibit 3 terminal balls reminding one of the pawnbroker's traditional symbol. Rootstocks are almost black, very slender, branched, and far-creeping, with the fronds arising so sparingly that dense mats are seldom formed. An inhabitant of moist, humus-rich, rocky mixed woods and, sometimes, swamp margins. Ranges from Newf. to Alaska and south to Va., Kans., and Colo. It is also found in forests of northern Europe and Asia. Tolerates a considerable range of soil acidity, apparently preferring about pH 4.0 to 5.0.

The oakfern is a delightful groundcover plant for the woodsgarden, and sends up its fronds so sparsely that it can be planted in every favorable spot without unduly crowding other plants. Spreading rapidly of its own accord, it may be propagated by rootstock cuttings, division, and from spores.

Crested Woodfern, Narrow Swampfern
(*Dryop'teris crista'ta*)

The fronds of this woodfern are very narrowly oval, pointed at the apex, twice-pinnate, and with the lower pinnae so short and broad as to be triangular. The 12 to 36 inch fertile, spore-bearing fronds (sporophyls) are much larger than the infer-

[163]

tile ones, and only the latter are evergreen. Frond stems are sparsely covered with light-brown papery scales, and spring in rather loose clusters from stout, scale-covered rootstocks. Pinnae are often turned to a horizontal position—an unusual habit, characteristic of this species. Fruit dots are small and covered with an umbrella-like roof, or 'indusium.'

Crested ferns grow rather plentifully in very wet woods, swampy thickets, and other soaking-wet (usually well-shaded) locations having mucky, moderately acid (pH 5–6) soil. They are wide-ranging, occurring in Europe, and in N.A. from Newfoundland to Idaho and south to N.C. and Ark.

The crested fern is an attractive woodsgarden plant, preferring a very wet spot, but also doing well with much less moisture. It multiplies by rootstock extension, and requires very little care.

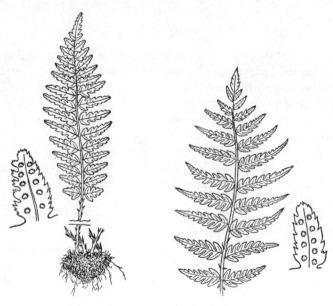

Dryopteris cristata   *Dryopteris clintoniana*

Clinton Woodfern, Broad Swampfern
(*Dryop'teris clintonia'na*)

Considerably larger than the crested woodfern, with fronds up to nearly 5 feet long, this species is otherwise very similar in

[164]

appearance, habitat, and cultivation. Moreover, it apparently hybridizes with and grades into the crested fern. However, in typical specimens fronds are broader, as well as larger, than those of *D. cristata*. Range is said to be N.H. to N.C. and west to Wis. pH 4–6.

Boott Woodfern (*Dryop'teris boott'i*)

Another relative of the crested woodfern, from which it is not readily distinguishable. Habitat and cultivation same, though this form is said to be more partial to swampy thickets than to wet woods. Range is said to be N.S. to Va. and west to Minn. pH 4–6.

Leather Woodfern, Marginal Woodfern
(*Dryop'teris margina'lis*)

A fine, upstanding fern, with dark, broadly oval, pointed, leathery, twice-pinnate, evergreen fronds from 12 to 36 inches tall. Pinnae heavily veined, with large, round, blue-black, umbrella-covered fruit dots (sori) at the very edges of the pinnules—hence the scientific and one of the common names. The very slowly creeping rootstock is upright, broad, and scale-covered; and each spring there rises from it an almost perfect vase-like circle of fronds, the stems of which are covered with lustrous light-brown scales.

This is a typically woodland fern, preferring nearly pure leafmold on ledges and boulder-strewn slopes, always well shaded. It is common in suitable locations, and is found from N.S. to Minn. and south to Ga., Ala., and Okla. Flourishes in acid, neutral, and even slightly alkaline soils. In our garden does well at about pH 4–5.

The leather woodfern should be in every woodsgarden, and can be propagated both by division and from spores. Likes an oakleaf wintercover (as do the other woodferns), and apparently has few insect or microbial enemies.

Toothed Woodfern (*Dryop'teris spinulo'sa*)

This group of woodferns, which includes the next two species, is distinguished from most others by their finely divided, lacy fronds, which appear early in the spring, from stout, rather short rootstocks. In this species the sterile fronds are evergreen,

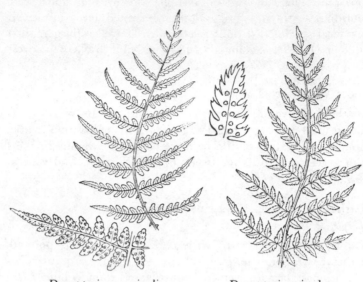

Dryopteris marginalis　　　　　*Dryopteris spinulosa*

but sporophyls (fertile fronds) wither by late fall. All fronds are relatively long and narrow, about 15 to 28 inches in length, and with the stem bearing pale-brown scales. The lower leafy parts of the fronds are twice-pinnate, the extreme upper parts once-pinnate; and the pinnules on the lower sides of the lowermost pinnae are longer than their opposite members. The pinnae, especially on the fertile fronds, slant upward from the stem. Fruit dots have smooth, light-brown, kidney-shaped covers (indusia) and turn shiny-black early in the season.

This is a very widespread species, ranging from Newfoundland westward, and south to N.C., Tenn., Ky., and Idaho. Occurs also in Europe and Asia. Prefers swamps, wet woods, and rocky slopes, in acid (pH 4.5–6), humus-rich soil. Cultivation easy. Relatively pest- and disease-free. Leafy winter-cover. Propagation by division or spores.

Common Woodfern (*Dryop'teris interme'dia*)

A very close relative of the preceding species, this woodfern has a cluster of 16 to 30 inch evergreen fronds from a coarse, erect

[166]

rootstock, with the crown of old plants extending well above-ground. The fronds are longer, narrower, and more finely divided than those of *D. spinulosa,* with the pinnae at right angles to the stem. Pinnules of the lowermost pinnae are deeply toothed. Young fronds and the fruit-dot covers (indusia) are covered with very fine sticky hairs. Frond stems bear light-brown scales, usually with darker centers. Fruit dots are small and located near the midribs of the pinnules. Although this is the commonest of our woodferns, it is not extremely wide-ranging—being found from Newf. and Wis. south to Ala. and Mo. Inclined to be a lowland form, it is abundant in moist, shady, preferably rocky woods with humus-rich soil, which may be acid, neutral, or slightly alkaline—pH 4.5 to 7.5.

Cultivation and propagation similar to those of the toothed woodfern.

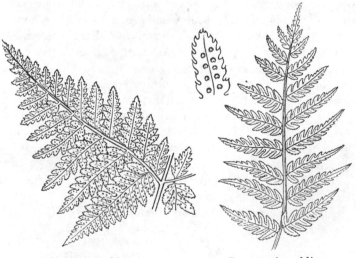

Dryopteris dilatata   Dryopteris goldiana

Mountain or Broad Woodfern (*Dryop'teris dilata'ta*)

A favorite for the woodsgarden, this fern is rather easily distinguished by its broad, 20 to 40 inch, non-evergreen fronds whose stems are plentifully sprinkled with large, dark-centered scales. Lowermost pinnae are triangular, with the lower

[167]

pinnules toothed and very much longer than the upper ones. Rootstock frequently nearly horizontal. Found in cool, rocky, upland woods and ravine slopes in very rich, strongly acid soil of pH 4–5. Ranges across Canada and south to N.C., Mich., and Wash. Common in Europe. Clute writes:

> This is the common form in Alaska. It is said that its rootstock is the first vegetable food the Alaska Indians are able to obtain in spring. It is dug before the fronds develop and baked in pits lined with hot stones.

Easily cultivatable in a very acid, humus-rich, moist, cool spot—preferably near a granite boulder.

Goldie or Giant Woodfern (*Dryop'teris goldia'na*)

This magnificent species is the largest of the woodferns, with fronds sometimes 48 inches long and a foot wide springing from a very heavy, creeping, horizontal, scale-tipped rootstock. The big, broadly oval fronds may be from yellow- to dark-green, are nearly twice-pinnate, and sharp-pointed. The new 'fiddle-heads' (crosiers) are covered with large pale-brown scales, as are the stems of the grown fronds. On the whole this fern looks much like a glorified marginal shield fern (leather woodfern), but its smaller fruit dots are near the centers, rather than at the margins, of the pinnules. Deep, cool, moist, humus-rich woods at moderate elevations. Said to prefer nearly neutral soil, but has done extremely well in our garden in a very acid location—pH 4.5. Ranges from southeastern Canada south and west to N.C., Tenn., Minn., and Iowa. Rare or absent in low coastal areas.

Cultivation and propagation similar to that of most other woodferns.

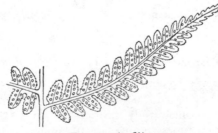

Dryopteris filixmas

Malefern (*Dryop'teris filixmas'*)

Superficially resembles *D. marginalis*, but the fruit dots are smaller and not at the edges of the pinnules, which are toothed; and the fronds are lighter green, widest above the middle, and not evergreen. Found in cold, rocky, acid (pH 4.5 to 6.0) woods from Newf. and N.S. south and west to Vt., Lakes Huron and Superior, N.D., and Ariz. Found also in Eurasia and South America. Difficult to cultivate, but has flourished, snuggled against a shaded granite ledge, in our garden.

Of this fern Clute writes:

> The stem and roots are bitter and astringent and have been used in lieu of hops in brewing. The ashes are reported to have been used in glass making. The curious 'St. John's hands' once sold to the credulous as charms against magic and witchcraft were made from the rootstock and unexpanded fronds of this species and the rootstock yields the Filixmas of the pharmacist. The last mentioned has been valued as a remedy for tapeworm since the time of Dioscorides. During the Middle Ages, its properties seem to have been forgotten for in the eighteenth century a certain Madam Mouffier is said to have sold the secret of its use to Louis XVI for 18,000 francs.

New York or Tapering Fern
(*Dryop'teris novaboracen'sis*)

This very common fern is easily identified by its narrowly oval, pointed, 8 to 24 inch fronds, whose pinnae are longest near the middle, and shorter and further apart toward the bottom, the lowermost being little more than greenish scales. Pinnae are divided into numerous narrow-roundish lobes. Fronds are yellow-green. Fertile fronds (sporophyls), not produced till summer, are somewhat longer and narrower than the sterile ones. Fruit dots (sori) are small but distinct, and are borne near the edges of the pinnae lobes. None of the fronds is evergreen. Their stems are pale green, and near their bases bear a few small, dark scales.

This is one of our most abundant ferns, preferring either moist or dry—more often the latter—woods of oak, beech, birch, and maple with humus-rich, somewhat acid soil of pH 4–6.0. In such locations its slender, branched rootstocks

[169]

creep extensively just below the groundlitter, sending up fronds singly or in tufts throughout the spring and summer, and sometimes forming a dense groundcover. Multiplication is so rapid that a short section of rootstock may in 2 or 3 years spread into a good-sized colony so dense as to crowd out other plants.

New York ferns range from Newf. to Minn. and south to Ga. and Ark. They are grand woodsgarden plants, nearly pest- and disease-free and of the easiest cultivation and propagation. Light leafy wintercover is desirable.

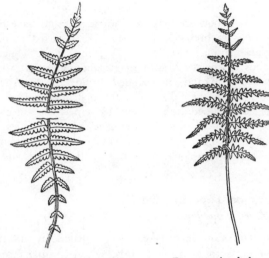

Dryopteris novaboracensis   *Dryopteris thelypteris*

Marshfern (*Dryop'teris thelyp'teris*) ·

This is not a woods fern, for it normally abounds in marshes and wet meadows, at bog margins, and in wet thickets. It does, however, sometimes occur in wet, open, deciduous woods. Its preference is for soft, moderately rich, acid (pH 4.5 to 6.5), muddy soil; and, although it prefers shade, it also does fairly well in full sun. The rootstock is cord-like, creeps extensively, and produces a row of grayish-green, deciduous, pointed-oval, 10 to 30 inch fronds with very long stems bronzy-brown below. Pinnae of sterile fronds, which appear early in the spring, are deeply divided into oval lobes. But the fertile fronds—usually

[170]

somewhat longer and narrower, and produced only during the summer—have, when mature, pinnae with triangular-shaped lobes with their edges folded over the mass of fruit dots on their under surfaces.

The immature fronds of this species, unfolding in earliest spring among the surrounding brown-seared vegetation, present a striking and characteristic mass of bright-green, curled-up balls which often attracts attention from a considerable distance.

Marsh ferns are found commonly from Newfoundland to at least Manitoba and south to Fla., La., and Okla. They occur widely, too, in Europe and Asia.

This fern does not belong in a woodsgarden unless there is a low, wet, semi-shaded spot to which it can be confined.

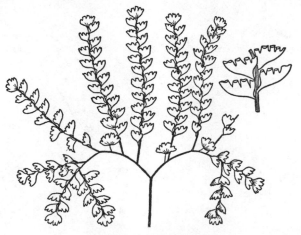

Adiantum pedatum

American or Northern Maidenhair (*Adian'tum peda'tum*)

This is one of our best-liked and most easily recognized ferns. Its delicate 8 to 20 inch fronds, with shiny, brownish-black stems, spread their pinnae horizontally in a nearly perfect circle. Rootstocks are dark, slender, branched, and creeping, and at intervals send up frond-clusters which are replenished throughout the summer. Uncurling young fronds (croziers) are covered with fine bluish hairs and their pinnae are red-tinted. Fruit dots are confined to the serrated edges of the pinnules, which fold over them to form covers (indusia).

The maidenhair is an exceedingly beautiful, and not at all uncommon, inhabitant of rich, moist woods, especially on northern exposures where the air is cool and humid. It grows well in a wide range of soils, but probably thrives best in slightly acid soil of pH 6–7. In the authors' gardens specimens have thrived for years at pH 4.5. Its range is wide: from N.S. to Alaska, and south to Ga., La., Mo., Utah, and Calif. Found in Asia, too.

This lovely species should be in every woodsgarden. It is exceedingly easy to grow, can be readily propagated by rootstock cuttings and from spores, and needs little protection except from snails and slugs.

Pteridium latiusculum

Eastern Bracken (*Pterid'ium latius'culum*)

Wherever the bracken grows it is conspicuous—and its distribution is almost worldwide.

Fronds are deciduous, triangular, thrice-pinnate, with the lowermost pair of primary pinnae so large as to resemble separate fronds. Stem brown toward the base and green above. Fronds up to more than 3 feet in height and nearly as broad as long. Fruit dots a continuous strip along the edges of the pinnules, which in-turn over them. Rootstock pencil-thick, branched, far-creeping, usually so deep as to escape damage from even serious forest fires. Sends up single fronds at intervals of inches or feet. Habitat open woods, pine barrens, roadsides, thickets, dry slopes, and sometimes bog margins. Usually prefers poor, very acid (pH 4–5) soil, but is occasionally found in rich, nearly neutral areas. Range of this species is from Newfoundland west, and south to at least Va., Miss., and Ariz. Other species or varieties (including a twice-pinnate variety found in sandy areas from Cape Cod to Fla. and Tex.) occur almost throughout North America.

Many myths and tales center around the bracken, and a number of them are interestingly told by Clute. The smoke from burning bracken was supposed to drive away 'serpents, gnats, and other noisome creatures'—and we, from our own experience, can testify that this fern makes an excellent smudge to ward off mosquitoes, black flies and no-see-ums. This same mysteriously powerful smoke was reputed to bring on rain; the briskly burning dry fronds have been used for calcining lime; and acid from green fronds was once used for tanning leather and in place of soap. Perhaps the strangest bracken-myth of all is that in ancient times, at dusk on midsummer eve, the bracken put forth a small blue flower which at midnight gave birth to a fiery seed which if caught in a white napkin conferred on its possessor the double gift of finding great treasure and donning a cloak of invisibility.

For centuries—probably for scores of thousands of years—this big fern has fed mankind in times of want. Throughout Europe it has been ground and mixed with flour in the ever-recurring famine periods. Indians of our own northwest have long feasted on the tremendous fronds of the local variety. Young croziers may be cooked and eaten like asparagus, and Volume 12 of the *American Botanist* gives several recipes for preparing them.

Bracken has no place in a small woodsgarden, for it is too large and quickly becomes weedy. But it is a grand groundcover for open woods having thin, humus-poor soil. The rootstock is claimed to be hard to transplant successfully, but we have found it appearing gratuitously in several of our gardens—and then have had a hard struggle to get rid of it. Nevertheless, it's a magnificent fern!

Hairy Lipfern (*Cheilan'thes lano'sa*)

The narrow, 6 to 10 inch, nearly evergreen fronds are brown-hairy, have short shiny-brown stems, and spring from a stumpy, slow-creeping rootstock, which is covered with hair-like brown scales. Fronds twice-pinnate, with pinnules deeply cut into roundish lobes. Fruit dots small and located near the outer ends of the lobes, which curl back to cover them partially. Habitat very dry crevices of sunny cliffs, ledges, and rocky slopes. During exceptionally dry weather the fronds curl upon themselves and appear nearly dead, but resume their color and posture with the first good rain. This is typically a southern fern, extending only as far northeastward as Connecticut. Westward it reaches Minn. and Wyo., and southward is found in Ga. and Tex. Over most of its range it prefers acid-forming rocks and soil of pH 5–6, but in southwestern areas may be found among limestone rocks where the soil is approximately neutral.

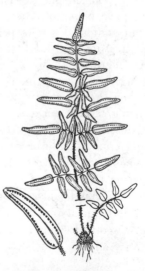

Cheilanthes lanosa   *Pellaea atropurpurea*

This is obviously not a woodsgarden fern, but is useful in the crevices of adjoining ledges. In the north it should be protected during the winter by an overturned berry basket.

Purple Cliffbrake (*Pellae'a atropurpu'rea*)

This unusual-colored fern has a short rootstock covered with whitish hairs that turn brown with age, bluish-green fronds, and frond stems of purplish-brown—from which it derives the first half of its common name. Fronds usually in loose clusters, once-pinnate near their upper ends and frequently twice-pinnate below. Fruit dots line the in-turned edges of the long, narrow pinnae and pinnules. Grows on dry limestone or sandstone cliffs, ledges and rocky slopes, usually in partial shade or full sun, in soil of about pH 6.5 to 7.5. Ranges, with nearly related species, from Canada to Fla. and westward.

Definitely not a woodland fern, but useful if your garden includes a limestone ledge.

Ebony Spleenwort (*Asple'nium platyneu'ron*)

A distinguishing characteristic of this fern is that its sterile and fertile fronds are entirely different in size, shape, color, and habit. The former are prostrate, only 2 to 6 inches long, have short-blunt, alternate pinnae, and are evergreen. Fertile fronds, on the other hand, are very narrowly oval, up to 24 inches long, stiffly erect, have a lustrous dark-brown stem, and bear short, alternate pinnae below and much longer, opposite, eared pinnae above. Fruit dots are hyphen-shaped (later spreading so as to cover most of the pinnae) and lie obliquely along the midveins. Rootstock short and erect, producing loose clusters of fronds and a mat of wiry black roots. Grows in gravelly soil on stony slopes and in open, rocky woods. Prefers only light shade. Indifferent to soil acidity, flourishing at about pH 5.0 to 7.5. Occurs from Me. and Colo. south to Fla. and Tex.

Maidenhair Spleenwort (*Asple'nium trichom'anes*)

This delightful little fern adorns shady ledges, cliffs, and caverns from N.S. to Alaska, and over most of the U.S. It is abundant, too, over much of Europe and Asia. The long, narrow, 2 to 8 inch evergreen fronds are all alike and spring in rosettes of from 10 to more than 100 from a short rootstock

[175]

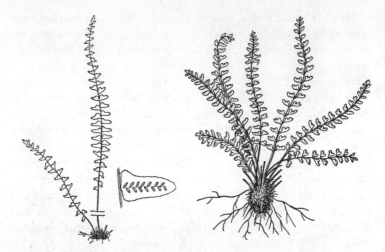

Asplenium platyneuron   *Asplenium trichomanes*

having a dense mass of wiry black roots. The stem, for its entire length, is dark, lustrous brown. Pinnae nearly opposite, oval or oblong, and notched on their upper edges. Fruit dots oval and placed obliquely in two rows.

This is one of our most dainty ferns, and certainly belongs in every woodsgarden that can give it a moist, shaded, ledgy lodging place. Cultivation and propagation—the latter by rootstock division—are easy. Soil acidity may be about anything you can offer: from pH 4.5 to 7.5. Protection must be provided against snails and slugs. An overturned berry basket furnishes desirable protection from winter and early spring winds. There are several nearly related species and varieties.

Ladyfern (*Athy'rium felixfem'ina*)

Noted fern experts do not agree on the description of this fern, for it is highly variable over its wide range in Europe, Asia, and North America. Some authorities claim that all the forms belong to this one species. Others split it up into several. *We* can't 'put a name' to all the variations, and we don't think you'll need to. We have followed *Standardized Plant Names* —and shall tell you about the *one* ladyfern. Later, perhaps, you can figure out the 'upland,' 'southern,' 'northern' species and their variations for yourself.

[176]

The fronds of the ladyfern spring in more or less dense tufts from a very heavy, horizontal, often only half-buried rootstock, and are usually from 2 to 3 feet long. In our experience, the fronds are twice-pinnate, with deeply toothed pinnules; and are widest several pinnae above the base. Stems may be greenish-yellow, reddish, or wine colored. Unfolding fronds (croziers) are characterized by a peculiarly angled—instead of smooth—curve, and vary considerably in color. Pinnules deeply toothed. Fruit dots narrowly kidney-shaped and when ripe either yellow-brown or blackish. Habitats of the several varieties (or species) vary considerably, for ladyferns are to be found abundantly in the full sun along dusty country roads, among the shaded rocks of moist deciduous woods, in swamps and wet thickets, and on brook banks. All the forms like humus-rich soil, of pH 4.5 to 6.5.

Athyrium felixfemina

Ladyferns are fine for the woodsgarden, though their dying fronds become unattractive early in the fall. If given plenty of water and protection from wind they are easy to cultivate and propagate—the latter by division or from spores.

Narrow-Leaf Spleenwort (*Athy'rium pycnocar'pon*)

This is a rare inhabitant of moist, cool, deciduous woods where the soil is humus-rich, deep, and nearly neutral (pH 6.5 to 7.5). The fronds are 20 to 40 inches tall, deciduous, brown-stemmed, scaly at their lower ends, pointed-oval, and once-pinnate. Fertile fronds are somewhat taller and narrower than the sterile ones, and do not appear till summer. Fruit dots linear, extending obliquely outward from the midveins of the pinnae. Rootstock rather coarse, creeping horizontally just below the groundlitter. Ranges from Que. to Wis., and south to Ga., La., and Mo.

Will do well in a suitable woodsgarden spot, but must have soil not more acid than pH 6.0.

Silvery Spleenwort (*Athy'rium thelypteroi'des*)

The 20 to 40 inch yellow-stemmed fronds of this fern somewhat resemble those of the ladyfern, but are only once-pinnate. Fruit dots silvery, narrow, and curved away from the midveins at an oblique angle. Habitat the rich, moderately acid (pH 5–6) soil of moist northern slopes, brook banks, and occasionally, open thickets. Ranges from N.S. to Minn., and south to Ga. and Mo. Found also in eastern Asia.

An excellent woodsgarden plant, having few enemies and easily propagated by division.

Hartstongue Fern (*Phylli'tis scolopen'drium*)

Although common in Europe, this is the rarest fern in North America, being found only at two locations in N.Y. and two in Canada. It is easily recognized by its long, narrow, unpinnated fronds, which, however, may be much distorted. Fruit dots are linear and extend outward from the central stem. Grows only in moist shade and nearly neutral soil (pH 6.5 to 7.5). Can be used in the woodsgarden (plants of European origin being obtainable from florists) and is easily propagated from spores.

Walking Fern (*Camptoso'rus rhizophyl'lus*)

This unusual and extremely interesting fern gets its name from the fact that the tapering 4 to 12 inch almost string-

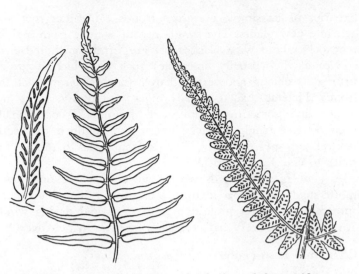

Athyrium pycnocarpon   *Athyrium thelypteroides*

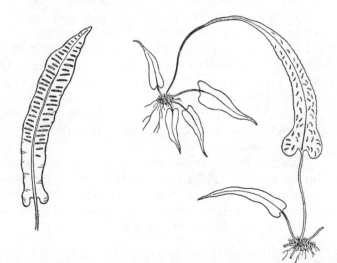

Phyllitis scolopendrium   *Camptosorus rhizophyllus*

like tips of its simple evergreen fronds sometimes root and generate new plants. The fronds rise in a circle from a short rootstock whose wiry black roots are firmly anchored in a crevice of the (usually limestone) rock on which it grows. Fruit dots oblong and scattered over the broader part of the fronds. Habitat shaded, usually moist and mossy, rocks and ledges and sometimes humus-rich hummocks—occasionally even on tree trunks. Prefers, but is not confined to, nearly neutral soil—pH 6.5 to 7.5. Ranges from Que. to Minn., and south to Ga., Kans., and Okla.

A gem in any woodsgarden, but cultivatable only on a moist, shady rock or ledge. In such locations it may flourish and spread, but requires protection from slugs and drying winds. An overturned berry basket makes excellent wintercover.

Christmas Fern (*Polys'tichum acrostichoi'des*)

One of our most common evergreen woodland ferns, found in humus-rich soil on rocky slopes, and less frequently in rock crevices, swamp hummocks, and thickets. Large masses of 12 to 30 inch evergreen fronds rise from a stout, slow-creeping rootstock early in the spring and while uncoiling are covered with fine white scales, which later turn brown and cover the lower stems till they wither the following spring. Fronds once-pinnate, with narrow, toothed pinnae eared at their inner ends. Fertile fronds taller than the sterile ones, with their upper pinnae both narrowed and shortened. Fruit dots usually, but not always, confined to the upper part of the fronds and, when ripe, practically covering the fertile area and coloring it brown. Some forms of this fern have broader fronds and more toothed pinnae.

This is a fine woodsgarden fern, easily grown in almost any humus-rich soil (pH 4.5 to 7.0) and good shade. Seems to be immune to disease and pests. Likes a light leafy wintercover, through which its young fronds easily force their way in spring. Multiplied by division of the clumps.

Mountain Hollyfern (*Polys'tichum lonchi'tis*)

This appropriately named near relative of the Christmas fern is evergreen and holly-like in appearance and *feel*. Its narrow, 4 to 20 inch, once-pinnate fronds spring in circular clumps from

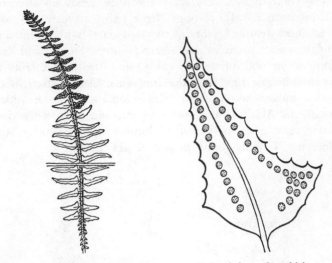

Polystichum acrostichoides   *Polystichum lonchitis*

a rootstock rather similar to, but smaller than, that of the Christmas fern. The fronds are stiff and short-stemmed, and the pinnae eared, scythe-shaped, prickly-toothed, and very short toward the lower end of the frond. Fruit dots in double rows on the upper pinnae, which are not so specialized as in the Christmas fern.

Mountain hollyfern is an inhabitant of northern regions around the world, occurring across Canada and southward to Wis., Utah, and Calif. Its favorite habitat is cold, rocky, limestone forests where the soil is deep, rich, and nearly neutral— pH 6.5 to 7.5. Although it does not occur naturally in our northeastern states it does well in woodsgardens there and can be purchased from wildflower dealers. Cultivation is not unduly difficult, but propagation (by division) is slow. Care is similar to that of the Christmas fern.

Braun Hollyfern (*Polys'tichum braun'i*)

Wherry calls this 'our most beautiful northern fern'; and in flourishing condition it is certainly an ornament to any woodsgarden—and not at all difficult to grow if an appropriate spot is available.

[181]

The short, heavy, very scaly rootstock sends up clusters of deciduous, narrowly oblong, densely brown-scaly, 18 to 30 inch, short-stemmed fronds, twice-pinnate, with pointed-oval pinnae whose pinnules are sharp-pointed. Sterile and fertile pinnules do not differ noticeably, and the round fruit dots are in a double row near the midveins. Occurs in rich, cool, usually upland woods from Newfoundland to Lake Superior (locally in Alaska), and south to Pa. and Wis. Very closely related ferns occur in British Columbia and the Rocky Mountain states. Usually found in soil of pH 6.0 to 7.5.

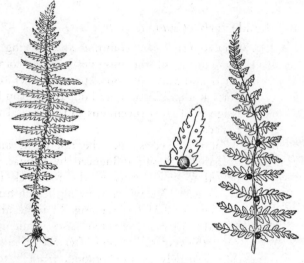

Polystichum brauni   *Cystopteris bulbifera*

Berry Bladderfern (*Cystop'teris bulbif'era*)

The long—up to 48 inches—very slender fronds of this graceful, rock-loving fern have short pinkish stems, are broadest at or near the lowest pinnae, and taper gradually to a slender point. Lower pinnae are divided into lobed pinnules, those next above have toothed pinnules, and the uppermost are merely lobed. Fronds pendant from cliffs or recumbent when the plant grows among rocks. Rootstock slender and creeping. Fruit dots round, small, and in a double row. Common name derived from bulblets borne on the under sides of the pinnae. These drop from the fronds and under favorable circumstances quickly

[182]

develop new plants. Sometimes the bulblets develop fronds of their own before dropping.

Habitat: moist shaded ledges, cliffs, and rocky slopes usually, but not always, of limestone. Preferred soil pH 6.5 to 7.5. Ranges from Newf. to Man. and south to Ga., Tenn., Wis., and Ariz.

Such an interesting woodsgarden fern that a suitable location may well be prepared for it by burying numerous limestone fragments in nearly neutral, humus-rich soil in a low, moist, heavily shaded area. Propagated by bulblets and rootstock division.

Brittle Bladderfern (*Cystop'teris frag'ilis*)

Of this fern Gray writes: ' . . . common and varying greatly in the shape and cutting of the pinnules.' Bailey comments: 'Widely distributed and variable.' So expect considerable difficulty in your efforts at identification; and do not, till you become expert, try to assign your own specimens to the several named-varieties of the species.

The rootstock of this species, like the rest of its anatomy, varies greatly, apparently being influenced by habitat. Where the fern is confined to small crevices, the rootstock may be short and relatively heavy; but when growing in rich humus of moist woods it is slender and far-creeping. In some areas the rootstock is scaly and bears many old stem bases, while in others the stems fall from the rootstocks soon after the fronds die.

The fronds are narrowly pointed-oblong, from 4 to more than 18 inches tall, loosely clustered, upright (except where they droop from cliff-faces), twice-pinnate, with slender stems brown below and green above. Pinnae rather pointed, usually with deeply toothed pinnules. Fruit dots small and round. Habitat varied: cliffs and ledges, rocky slopes, and open deciduous woods—preferably moist and shaded. Range extraordinarily wide: Greenland to Alaska, and south to Ga., Ala., and Calif.; and 'reported from South Africa, India, Ethiopia, New Zealand, and the Hawaiian Islands' (Clute).

One of the earliest spring ferns, with fronds withering during drouths and quickly replaced after the next rainy spell. Generally prefers intimate contact with limey rocks and nearly neutral (pH 6.5 to 7.5) soil, but has done well for years in our

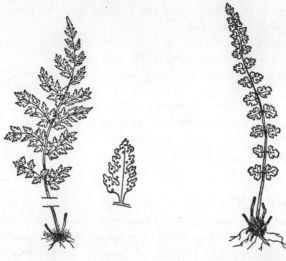

Cystopteris fragilis   Woodsia glabella

garden in strongly acid (pH 4.5) humus-rich soil under pines and on semi-shaded granite ledges. An interesting woods- or ledge- garden plant, individual specimens preferably being given approximately the same conditions in which they originally grew. Hardy and disease-resistant, but may require protection from snails. Propagation by division.

Smooth Woodsia (*Wood'sia glabel'la*)

This rare little rock-embracing fern is principally distinguished by its exceedingly narrow once-pinnate fronds and short, bluntly-lobed pinnae. Rootstock tiny. Fruit dots small, mostly on outer portion of lobes.. Habitat: rocks—preferably moist, mossy, and limey, with soil reaction probably from pH 6.5 to 7.5. Range: Greenland and Newfoundland to Alaska, and south to N.E. and N.Y. Also Eurasia. So rare in N.E. that it should not be collected unless one's woodsgarden presents exactly the right habitat.

Rusty Woodsia (*Wood'sia ilven'sis*)

Usually easy to identify by its small, 2 to 6 inch, thickish fronds, dark-green above and densely covered below with rusty-brown,

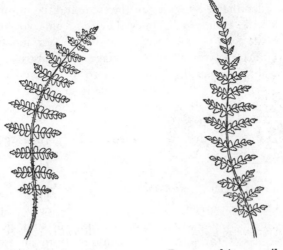

Woodsia ilvensis   *Dennstaedtia punctilobula*

bristle-like chaff. Fronds twice-pinnate, pinnae crowded and oblong, pinnules bluntly oval, fruit dots near lobe-margins and nearly touching when old. Frond stems usually brownish below, greenish among the pinnae, and jointed so that when broken from the plant, stubble of uniform length is left on the root-stock, which is short and covered with a dense mass of fine roots. Grows always in contact with rocks—on ledges, cliffs, and rocky slopes—frequently in extremely dry locations in full sun. Soil usually moderately acid (pH 5–6). Occurs in cold northern areas in North America, Europe, and Asia. In the U.S. it ranges south, in the mountains, through N.E. to N.C. and some western states.

This is one of the finest plants for a granite ledge. In our garden one specimen, tightly wedged into a narrow crack in an exposed granite ledge, grew so rapidly that we secured 9 husky divisions—just by slicing the original fern into pieces—in one year. Completely deciduous in New England; but said to be evergreen farther south. No special care, except frequent watering in dry spells.

Common Woodsia (*Wood'sia obtu'sa*)

Difficult for the beginner to differentiate from the brittle bladder-fern, but identifiable by scales on the stem and the minute hairs that cover the frond; pale- or yellowish-green color of stem; blunt, rather than pointed, pinnae and pinnules; and fruit-dot covers (indusia) which at one stage of maturity become recognizably star-shaped. Fronds 6 to 16 inches; and rootstock very short. Found on sheltered, usually limey, cliffs, rocks, and rocky slopes in southeastern Canada, south to Ga., and west to Wis. and Ariz. (Clute).

Good for a well-drained, shaded, rocky garden spot with soil of about pH 6.0 to 7.5.

Hay-Scented Fern (*Dennstaed'tia punctilob'ula*)

The delicate, light-green, 18 to 36 inch fronds are twice-pinnate, sharp-pointed, thin-textured, brown-stemmed, and generated in dense masses throughout the summer from an extensive, wide-ranging rootstock. Herbage minutely hairy and with numerous glands secreting a hay-scented wax. Fruit dots tiny, usually one at the base of each pinnule notch. Sterile, rocky, hillside pastures and dry open woods, in full sun or partial shade, and acid soil of pH 4.5 to 6.0. N.S. and Minn. to Ga., Ala., and Ark.

A very attractive fern, hardy and quick-spreading, preferably nestled against a granite boulder, and requiring rigid control.

Sensitive Fern (*Onocle'a sensib'ilis*)

This is definitely a weedy fern and should be rigidly excluded from any but the largest and wettest woodsgardens. It varies from a few inches to more than 3 feet high, the sterile and fertile fronds being entirely different. The former may be from light to brown-mottled green, and are deeply cut into long wavy-edged lobes which do not quite reach the stem. Fertile fronds appear in late summer and are twice-pinnate, with the pinnules rolled into globular receptacles around the spore cases. While the sterile fronds wither early, the stiff fertile ones, though dead, remain upright throughout the winter. Rootstock pencil-thick, branching, and far-creeping on or near the surface. Thrives in muddy soil varying from pH 4.5 to 7.5.

[186]

Onoclea sensibilis

Occurs abundantly in swamps, meadows, thickets, and wet woods—being equally at home in full sun or partial shade. Found in Eurasia; and from Newfoundland across Canada, south to the Gulf and west at least to the Mississippi River.

Ostrich Fern (*Ptere'tis nodulo'sa*)

This is really not a woodland fern, but is so beautiful and plentiful that it must be included anyway!

Sterile fronds 2 to 8 feet tall, once-pinnate, tapered at both base and apex, brown-stemmed, and slightly scaly. Lobes on pinnae not toothed. Fertile fronds entirely different: pinnate, autumnal, relatively short, and with edges of pinnae in-turned to form a beaded plume persistent through the winter. Rootstock thick, creeping, branched, and producing urn-like clusters of fronds from scaly, terminal heads, which may project several inches above the surface. At its best in the midwest in the sandy soil along streams. 'In the northern United States there are many jungle-like thickets of this species in which a man of ordinary height may stand and be completely hidden' (Clute). Occurs also in swamps, wooded flats, and humus-rich rocky woods and thickets—in either full sun or partial shade, and in soil of pH 5.0 to 7.5. Ranges from Newfoundland to Alaska, and south to Va. and Iowa. Found also in Europe.

[187]

Pteretis nodulosa

Does well in a semi-shaded spot in the woodsgarden, if given humus-rich, sandy, nearly neutral soil. Robust, but benefits from frequent watering. May require forceful restraint.

Hartford or Climbing Fern (*Lygo'dium palma'tum*)

This is our only representative of the true climbing ferns, one of which is said to have fronds up to 50 feet long.

The Hartford fern does not, at first glance, seem at all fernlike. The fronds consist of a much-elongated, string-like, dark-brown stem, 18 to 40 inches long, from which twin palm-shaped 'leaves' diverge at considerable intervals. The fronds spring from a delicate, far-creeping rootstock, and twine loosely around available upright vegetation, or lie prone. Fertile fronds are like others, except that their upper ends are repeatedly pinnate and devoted exclusively to spore-bearing. With the arrival of fall the fertile areas wither; but the rest of the fronds are evergreen. Habitat moist, very acid (pH 4–5), partly shaded thickets, bogs, and open woods. Occurs, abundantly, at isolated locations from N.H. to Fla., Tenn., Ky., and Ohio.

Attractive in cultivation, but we have found it difficult to establish. Requires protection from wind and snails.

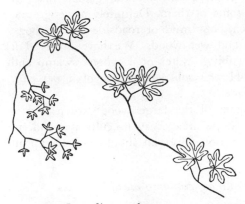

Lygodium palmatum

Osmunda regalis

Royal Fern (*Osmun'da rega'lis*)

This imposing and beautiful fern well deserves its name, for its delicate fronds, sometimes 6 feet long and crowned with flower-seeming, fruiting pinnae, are worth traveling far to see—but are common over much of North and South America, Europe, Asia, and Africa. Rootstock very heavy, compound and erect, sometimes forming a circular mound a foot high. 'Fiddle-heads' (young, uncoiling fronds; croziers) brown-wooly, later dropping the wool and revealing the 'wine-colored petioles with their burden of pink or ochre pinnae' (Clute).

Mature fronds bright green except for the golden mass of fertile pinnae topping some of them. Definitely a wet-ground fern, preferring the rich, oozy mud of roadside ditches, bogs, swamps, streambanks, and wet woods. We have observed it in the extremely acid (pH 4) water of a cypress swamp and in slightly alkaline (pH 7.5) soil at the base of a wet cliff. Prefers sun or light shade.

A truly regal inhabitant of the large woodsgarden with a lightly shaded, semi-swampy area. Easy to cultivate; and, in most areas, there is no reason why you should not dig up all you need.

Cinnamon Fern (*Osmun'da cinnamo'mea*)

One of our largest, commonest, and—just before the spores ripen—most beautiful ferns. Unfortunately it becomes sear and unattractive rather early in the fall. Dead fronds should then be removed promptly.

Rootstocks are heavy and compound, often forming dense, brush-like masses several feet in circumference and giving rise to half a dozen or more groups of fronds. 'Fiddle-heads' (very young, uncoiling fronds, or croziers) appear in early spring, and are at first covered with a dense white fuzz, which later turns brown and drops off. It is a favorite nesting material for certain small birds. Sterile and fertile fronds are entirely different in this species. The fertile ones appear first, growing from the outer part of the crown. They are thick-stemmed, erect, stiff, and covered with specialized pinnae, which turn their upper portions into a thick spike of fruit dots—at first bright green, then golden brown (whence the common name), and finally a dark chocolate as the stalk withers away before summer ends. Sterile fronds, spring from the inner part of the rootstock crown, bend sharply outwards, and form a vase-shaped circle enclosing the 'cinnamon' stalks. Sterile fronds of this species can always be distinguished from those of the next species by the tiny tuft of fuzz on the back of the base of each pinna. Reaches a height of 6 feet. Abundant in marshes, thickets, wet fields, open woods, and roadside ditches—always in muddy soil, which may be from very (pH 4) to slightly acid (pH 6.5). Range: Eurasia, South America, West Indies, and eastern North America south to southern Fla. Some plants growing in deep woods have pinkish frond stems.

Does well in a wet, very lightly shaded garden, and is fool-proof in cultivation. Undeveloped fronds in the crowns of this and the next species are often eaten boiled or as a salad, and are tasty and nutritious.

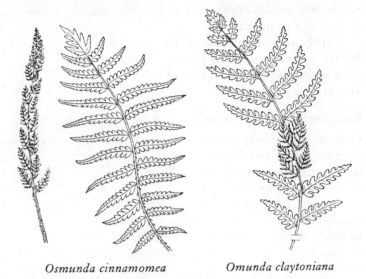

Osmunda cinnamomea   Omunda claytoniana

Interrupted Fern (*Osmun'da claytonia'na*)

Except for a difference in fertile fronds and the lack of a fuzzy tuft at the base of each pinna, this species is very similar to the *O. cinnamo'mea,* whose range and habitat it shares to a great extent. In its fertile fronds, which are somewhat longer than the others, 2 to 5 pairs of the pinnae are themselves twice-pinnate and utilized solely for spore-bearing—a unique characteristic of the species, and the source of its common name. Habitat much the same as that of the cinnamon fern, but includes dry situations and somewhat less acid or even neutral soils. Range, eastern North America, West Indies, South America, and Asia.

A good woodsgarden plant, requiring some sun. Foolproof, and needing little care.

Common Grapefern (*Botry'chium obli'quum*)

This and the other grapeferns bear only a single thickish frond, which is divided near the ground to form sterile and fertile

Botrychium obliquum

portions. The former is twice-pinnate, with the lowest pinnae greatly enlarged and triangular. The fertile branch is very long-stemmed and at its apex bears highly specialized pinnae devoted exclusively to bearing grape-like spore cases filled with golden-yellow spores. 'Leaf' evergreen, turning bronzy in fall and functioning till the new frond appears late the following July. Spores ripen in September, and their part of the frond soon withers and disappears. Rootstock short, erect, and fleshy-rooted, with next year's bud developing in the hollow base of this year's frond. Found in damp thickets, old pastures, wet open woods, and along stone fences, from N.B., Ont., and Minn. south to Fla., Tenn., and Mo.

This and other grapeferns are interesting, though inconspicuous, woodsgarden plants, preferring fairly humus-rich acid soil (pH 5–6), light shade, frequent watering, protection from cutworms and slugs, and very little wintercover. Easy to transplant if their roots are not disturbed.

Cutleaf Grapefern (*Botry'chium dissec'tum*)

This species, except for a somewhat more finely divided 'leaf,' so

[192]

closely resembles the common grapefern in appearance, habits, habitat, range, and cultural requirements that it needs no further description here.

Broadleaf Grapefern (*Botry'chium multif'idum*)

Another species so closely resembling the common grapefern that it requires little mention here. 'Leaf' somewhat less divided and more leathery, appearing earlier and not turning bronzy in fall. Range mostly north of the U.S.

Botrychium virginianum

Rattlesnake Fern (*Botry'chium virginia'num*)

Largest of the grapefern group, sometimes reaching a height of 3 feet, this fern is easily distinguished from the preceding species by the fact that the fertile stalk is really a continuation of the main stem and rises from between the lowermost pinnae of the 'leaf.' Frond appears early in the spring and lasts through the summer, though the fertile portion withers earlier. Not evergreen. Habitat principally dense deciduous woods with deep, humus-rich soil, which may be anywhere from strongly acid to neutral (pH 4.5 to 7.0). Ranges over northern Europe, Asia, and North America, having a wide range in the U.S.

One of the best woodsgarden ferns, but must have proper soil, plenty of water, and protection from slugs, cutworms, and drying winds. Wintercover preferably of oak and beech leaves, left in place in spring. Propagation by spores. Stalk very brittle, requiring great care in collecting.

THE FERN ALLIES

This ancient group of non-flowering, spore-bearing plants are called 'fern allies' because they have so many fern-like character-istics. There are several sub-groups, but the only one with which the woodsgardener need be concerned is known as the Clubmoss Family and includes the clubmosses, ground pines, and the ground cedars—which are neither mosses, pines, nor cedars except to the highly imaginative casual observer who is likely to know them best as Christmas decorations.

All of this sub-group of plants are creeping, with long, branched, sparse-rooted surface or near-surface stems. They are extremely difficult to reproduce from spores but, with due precaution, can be readily brought to your garden and there propagated by means of stem cuttings, which must include upright branches or terminal buds and at least a few roots. The cuttings must be kept damp till re-planted, and thereafter till thoroughly established, and will not thrive unless watered frequently and protected from direct sunlight and drying winds. An overturned berry basket helps.

Most of the woods-loving species prefer dense shade, very acid (pH 4.0 to 5.0), humus-rich soil, plenty of groundlitter, and a light needle or leaf wintercover. Before taking individual plants from the woods, study their surroundings carefully, and in your garden give them conditions as nearly as practical like their natural habitat.

The accompanying sketches will enable you to differentiate between clubmosses, ground pines, and ground cedars; and you need not bother about any more detailed identification.

Typical clubmoss

Typical ground pine

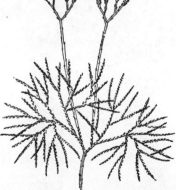

Typical ground cedar

Soil Reaction Requirements

Scientific and Common Names	4–5	5–6	6–7	7–8
Actaea alba (white baneberry)		x		
Actaea rubra (red baneberry)		x		
Adiantum pedatum (American maidenhair fern)		x	x	
Adlumia fungosa (mountain-fringe)		x		
Agrimonia striata (roadside agrimony)		x		
Allium canadense (Canada garlic)			x	
Allium triccoccum (wild leek)			x	
Amianthium muscaetoxicum (crowpoison)	x			
Anemone canadensis (meadow anemone)			x	
Anemone quinquefolia (wood anemone)		x		
Anemone virginiana (Virginia anemone)		x	x	
Anemonella thalictroides (rue anemone)	x	x		
Aplectrum hyemale (puttyroot orchid)			x	
Apocynum androsaemifolium (spreading dogbane)		x		
Aquilegia canadensis (American columbine)		x	x	
Aralia nudicaulis (wild sarsaparilla)		x		
Arisaema dracontium (green dragon)			x	
Arisaema triphyllum (jack-in-the-pulpit)		x		
Aristolochia durior (Dutchmanspipe)			x	
Asarum canadense (Canada wildginger)	x	x		
Asplenium platyneuron (ebony spleenwort)		x	x	x
Asplenium trichomanes (maidenhair spleenwort)		x	x	x
Aster acuminatus (acuminate aster)		x		
Aster divaricatus (white wood aster)		x	x	
Aster lateriflorus (calico aster)	x	x		
Aster umbellatus (flat-top aster)		x		
Atherium felixfemina (ladyfern)	x	x	x	
Atherium pycnocarpon (narrow-leaf spleenwort)			x	x
Atherium thelypteroides (silvery spleenwort)		x		

Scientific and Common Names	Preferred pH			
	4–5	5–6	6–7	7–8
Aureolaria glauca (oakleech)	x			
Aureolaria pedicularia (oakleech)	x			
Azalea canescens (Piedmont)	x			
Azalea lutea (flame)	x			
Azalea nudiflora (pinxterbloom)	x	x		
Botrychium dissectum (cutleaf grapefern)		x		
Botrychium multifidum (broadleaf grapefern)		x		
Botrychium obliquum (common grapefern)		x		
Botrychium virginianum (rattlesnake fern)	x	x		
Caltha palustris (marsh-marigold)		x	x	
Calypso bulbosa (calypso)		x		
Camassia esculenta (Atlantic camas)			x	
Campanula americana (American bluebell)			x	
Camptosorus rhizophyllus (walking fern)			x	x
Cardamine douglassi (Douglass bittercress)			x	x
Caulophyllum thalictroides (blue cohosh)		x	x	x
Ceanothus americanus (Jerseytea)			x	
Chamaelirium luteum (fairywand)		x		
Cheilanthes lanosa (hairy lipfern)		x		
Chimaphila maculata (striped pipsissewa)	x			
Chimaphila umbellata (common pipsissewa)	x			
Cimicifuga racemosa (cohosh bugbane)		x		
Claytonia caroliniana (Carolina spring-beauty)		x		
Claytonia virginica (Virginia spring-beauty)		x		
Clematis virticillaris (rock clematis)			x	
Clintonia borealis (beadlily)	x			
Clintonia umbellulata (speckled beadlily)		x		
Collinsonia canadensis (citronella horsebalm)			x	
Collinsia verna (blue-eyed-Mary)			x	
Conopholis americana (squawroot)	x	x		
Coptis groenlandica (goldthread)	x			

Scientific and Common Names	Preferred pH			
	4–5	5–6	6–7	7–8
Corallorrhiza maculata (spotted coralroot)			x	
Corallorrhiza odontorhiza (late coralroot)		x		
Corallorrhiza striata (hooded coralroot)			x	
Corallorrhiza trifida (early coralroot)		x		
Cornus canadensis (bunchberry)	x			
Corydalis aurea (golden corydalis) ⸱			x	
Corydalis sempervirens (pale corydalis)		x		
Cyprepedium acaule (pink ladyslipper)	x			
Cyprepedium arietinum (ramshead ladyslipper)		x		
Cyprepedium candidum (white ladyslipper)			x	x
Cyprepedium parviflorum (small yellow ladyslipper)		x		
Cyprepedium parviflorum pubescens (large yellow ladyslipper)		x	x	
Cyprepedium reginae (showy ladyslipper)		x	x	
Cystopteris bulbifera (berry bladderfern)			x	x
Cystopteris fragilis (brittle bladderfern)		x	x	x
Dalibarda repens (star-violet)	x			
Delphinium exaltatum (tall larkspur)			x	
Dennstaedtia punctilobula (hay-scented fern)	x	x		
Dentaria diphylla (crinkleroot toothwort)		x		
Dentaria laciniata (cutleaf toothwort)			x	
Dicentra canadensis (squirrel-corn)			x	
Dicentra cucullaria (Dutchmansbreeches)			x	
Dicentra eximia (fringed bleedingheart)	x	x		
Disporum lanuginosum (hairy fairybells)			x	x
Dodecatheon meadia (shooting star)	x	x		
Dryopteris booti (Boott woodfern)	x	x		
Dryopteris clintoniana (Clinton woodfern)	x	x		
Dryopteris cristata (crested woodfern)	x	x		
Dryopteris dilatata (mountain woodfern)	x			
Dryopteris disjuncta (oakfern)	x			
Dryopteris filixmas (malefern)	x	x		
Dryopteris goldiana (Goldie woodfern)	x	x	x	
Dryopteris hexagonoptera (broad beechfern)	x			
Dryopteris intermedia (common woodfern)		x	x	x
Dryopteris marginalis (leather woodfern)		x		
Dryopteris novaboracensis (New York fern)	x	x		
Dryopteris phegopteris (narrow beechfern)	x	x		
Dryopteris spinulosa (toothed woodfern)	x	x		
Dryopteris thelypteris (marshfern)	x	x	x	
Epifagus virginiana (beechdrops)	x	x		

	4–5	5–6	6–7	7–8
Epigaea repens (trailing-arbutus)	x			
Epilobium angustifolium (fireweed)			x	
Erigenia bulbosa (harbinger-of-spring)			x	
Erythronium albidum (white fawnlily)			x	
Erythronium americanum (common fawnlily)		x		
Eupatorium rugosum (white snakeroot)			x	
Frasera carolinensis (Caroline frasera)			x	
Galium boreale (northern bedstraw)		x	x	
Gaultheria procumbens (checkerberry wintergreen)	x	x		
Geranium maculatum (wild geranium)		x	x	
Geranium robertianum (herbrobert geranium)			x	
Gillenia stipulata (Bowman-root)		x		
Gillenia trifoliata (Indian-physic)		x		
Goodyera pubescens (downy rattlesnake-plantain)		x		
Goodyera repens (lesser rattlesnake-plantain)	x			
Goodyera tesselata (checkered rattlesnake-plantain)	x			
Habenaria ciliaris (yellow fringe-orchid)		x		
Habenaria hookeri (Hooker orchid)	x			
Habenaria orbiculata (padleaf orchid)		x		
Habenaria rotundifolia (roundleaf orchid)	x			
Habenaria v. bracteata (satyr orchid)	x			
Helianthus divaricatus (divaricate sunflower)			x	x
Hepatica acutiloba (sharplobe hepatica)			x	
Hepatica americana (roundlobe hepatica)	x	x		
Heuchera americana (American alumroot)			x	
Hexalectris spicata (crested coralroot)			x	
Hydrastis canadensis (goldenseal)			x	
Hydrophyllum appendiculatum (waterleaf)			x	
Hydrophyllum virginianum (Virginia waterleaf)			x	
Hypericum ascyron (giant St. Johnswort)		x		
Hypopitys latisquama (pinesap)	x			
Hypoxis hirsuta (goldstar grass)	x			
Jeffersonia diphylla (American twinleaf)	x	x	x	
Kalmia latifolia (mountain laurel)	x	x		

Scientific and Common Names	Preferred pH			
	4-5	5-6	6-7	7-8
Lilium philadelphicum (wood lily)	x			
Linnaea borealis (twinflower)	x			
Linum virginianum (woodland flax)			x	
Liparis liliifolia (lily twayblade)	x			
Lonicera sempervirens (trumpet honeysuckle)		x		
Luzula campestris (woodrush)			x	
Lygodium palmatum (Hartford fern)	x			
Maianthemum canadense (beadruby)	x			
Medeola virginiana (Indian cucumber-root)	x			
Mertensia virginica (Virginia bluebells)			x	
Mitchella repens (partridgeberry)	x			
Mitella diphylla (miterwort)		x	x	
Monarda didyma (Oswego beebalm)			x	
Monotropa uniflora (Indian-pipe)		x		
Nothoscordum bivalve (yellow false garlic)			x	
Obolaria virginica (Virginia pennyleaf)		x		
Onoclea sensibilis (sensitive fern)	x	x	x	x
Orchis spectabilis (showy orchis)		x	x	
Osmunda cinnamomea (cinnamon fern)	x	x		
Osmunda claytoniana (interrupted fern)		x		
Osmunda regalis (royal fern)	x	x		
Oxalis montana (American woodsorrel)	x			
Oxalis violacea (violet woodsorrel)			x	
Panax quinquefolium (American ginseng)	x	x		
Panax trifolium (dwarf ginseng)		x	x	
Pedicularis canadensis (early pedicularis)		x	x	
Pellaea atropurpurea (purple cliffbrake)			x	x
Phacelia purshi (Pursch phacelia)			x	x
Phlox divaricata (sweet-William phlox)			x	
Phyllitis scolopendrium (hartstongue fern)			x	x
Phytolacca americana (pokeberry)		x		

Scientific and Common Names	Preferred pH			
	4–5	5–6	6–7	7–8
Podophyllum peltatum (mayapple)	x	x	x	
Pogonia affinis (fullcrest pogonia)	x			
Pogonia trianthophora (drooping pogonia)			x	
Pogonia verticillata (Atlantic pogonia)	x			
Polemonium reptans (creeping polemonium)			x	
Polygala paucifolia (fringed polygala)	x			
Polygonatum biflorum (small solomonseal)	x	x		
Polygonatum commutatum (great solomonseal)	x	x		
Polygonatum major giganteum (giant solomonseal)			x	
Polypodium polypodioides (resurrection fern)	x			
Polypodium vulgare (common polypody)	x	x		
Polystichum acrostichoides (Christmas fern)	x	x	x	
Polystichum brauni (Braun hollyfern)			x	x
Polystichum lonchitis (mountain hollyfern)			x	x
Pteretis nodulosa (ostrich fern)			x	x
Pteridium latiusculum (eastern bracken)	x			
Pyrola americana (American pyrola)	x	x		
Pyrola elliptica (waxflower pyrola)	x	x		
Ranunculus hispidus (bristly buttercup)			x	
Rhexia virginica (meadow-beauty)	x			
Rhododendron maximum (rose-bay)	x	x		
Rhododendrons (various kinds)	x	x		
Rhodora canadensis (rhodora)	x	x		
Rubus odoratus (thimbleberry)		x		
Rudbeckia laciniata (cutleaf coneflower)		x	x	
Sanguinaria canadensis (bloodroot)		x	x	
Silene stellata (starry silene)		x	x	
Silene virginica (firepink silene)		x	x	
Smilacina racemosa (starry solomonplume)		x		
Smilacina stellata (solomonplume)		x		
Solidago bicolor (silver goldenrod)		x		
Solidago caesia (wreath goldenrod)		x	x	
Solidago flexicaulis (zigzag goldenrod)		x		
Solidago juncea (plume goldenrod)		x		
Solidago odora (fragrant goldenrod)	x	x		
Solidago speciosa (noble goldenrod)			x	

Scientific and Common Names	Preferred pH			
	4–5	5–6	6–7	7–8
Stenanthium graminium (featherfleece)	x			
Streptopus amplexifolius (claspleaf twistedstalk)		x		
Streptopus roseus (rosy twistedstalk)		x		
Stylophorum diphyllum (celandine poppy)			x	
Symplocarpus foetidus (skunkcabbage)		x	x	
Thalesia uniflora (ghostpipe)		x		
Tiarella cordifolia (foamflower)			x	x
Tipularia unifolia (cranefly orchid)	x			
Tradescantia virginiana (spiderlily)			x	
Trientalis borealis (American starflower)	x			
Trillium cernuum (nodding trillium)		x		
Trillium erectum (purple trillium)	x			
Trillium grandiflorum (white trillium)			x	
Trillium nivale (dwarf trillium)			x	x
Trillium undulatum (painted trillium)	x			
Uvularia grandiflora (big merrybells)			x	
Uvularia sessilifolia (little merrybells)		x		
Violaceae (table of kinds)	x	x	x	
Waldsteinia fragarioides (barren strawberry)		x		
Woodsia glabella (smooth woodsia)			x	x
Woodsia ilvensis (rusty woodsia)		x		
Woodsia obtusa (common woodsia)			x	x
Xerophyllum asphodeloides (turkeybeard)			x	

Glossary

Acid: With reference to soils—'sour'; having a pH number under about 6.
Acuminate: Tapering to a point.
Alkaline: With reference to soils—'sweet'; having a pH number above 7.
Alternate: An arrangement of leaves, buds, pinnae, etc. spaced alternately—not oppositely—along a stem.
Annual: Having a one-year life-cycle.
Axil: Angle between the upper side of a leaf- or stem-stalk or a branch and its supporting stem or other branch.
Bacterium (plural, *bacteria*): A simple form of microscopic nongreen vegetable organism.
Biennial: Having a life-cycle of two years.
Clasping: Referring to a stalkless leaf whose base at least partly surrounds the stem from which it springs.
Compost: A mixture of various substances (e.g. leaves, other vegetation, and manure) undergoing decay, for addition to garden soils.
Compost pile: A pile of leaves, other vegetable matter, manure, etc. undergoing decomposition into compost.
Compound: Used herein to describe a leaf or frond naturally cut into several parts.
Coniferous: Cone-bearing (e.g. pines, hemlocks, spruces, firs, larches, cypresses, cedars, etc.). Mostly evergreen trees.
Corm: An enlarged, fleshy, usually underground base of a stem.
Crozier: An uncoiling frond.
Deciduous: Shedding leaves each winter.
Division: A form of plant propagation in which new individuals are produced by separation from the parents.
Fiddle-head: A very young crozier.
Frond: The entire leafy portion of a fern, including the stem.
Fruit-dot: A group of tiny capsules bearing spores.
Fungus (plural, *fungi, funguses*): A relatively large, usually visible, form of nongreen plant.
Genus: Group of plants made up of sub-groups of species.
Germinate: To sprout and put forth roots.
Groundlitter: Miscellaneous material topping the forest floor.
Habitat: The surroundings in which a given kind of plant or animal grows.
Hardpan: The lowest level of soil.
Herb: A plant that annually dies to the ground, as distinguished from shrubs and other plants with woody stems living from year to year.
Herbaceous: Herb-like; not woody.
Host: An organism that harbors a parasite.
Humus: Partially decomposed vegetable and/or animal matter.
Indusium: The cover of a fruit-dot.

[205]

Inorganic: Mineral soil ingredients not having the characteristics of living bodies (e.g. sand).

Lath-house: A shade-house having roof and/or sides made of spaced laths.

Leafmold: Decomposed leaves.

Leaf-rosette: A cluster of leaves, usually on the ground.

Leaf-scale: A small rudimentary or specialized leaf, frequently without green coloring matter.

Leaf-whorl: A circular arrangement of leaves.

Lobe: A small division of a leaf or frond, bounded by notches that do not extend as far as the stem.

Marl Soil: A soil consisting largely of limey clay.

Micro-organism: A microscopic plant or animal.

Mold: Loose, extremely humus-rich soil. Includes leafmold and needlemold.

Muck: Very rich dark brown or black soil consisting largely of ancient plant materials further decomposed than peat or humus.

Mulch: Loose material—such as leaves, leafmold, shredded peat, etc.— spread on ground to keep it cool and moist and to add, through gradual decomposition, to its humus content.

Needlemold: Decomposed needles of pines, spruces, and other coniferous trees.

Neutral: With reference to soils—neither acid nor alkaline.

Node: That part of a stem at which leaves and buds have their origin.

Nomenclature: A system of names or terms.

Organic Material: Substances characteristic of, or derived from, living organisms (e.g. humus).

Ovary: That part of a flower within which eggs (ovules) are formed.

Ovate: Used to describe a plant part that is narrow at the base, considerably wider toward the middle, and pointed at the tip.

Peat, peat moss: Ancient, partly decomposed sphagnum moss, dug, dried, and shredded.

Perennial: Plant having a life-cycle of more than two years.

Petals: The inner set of floral leaves which make up a flower.

Pinna (plural, *pinnae*): A primary division of a compound fern frond, with openings between pinnae extending clear to the stem.

Pinnate: Divided into leaflets (pinnae) arranged along a common stem.

Pinnule: A secondary, or tertiary, pinna.

Pollen: The fertilizing agent of flowering plants.

Pollination: The transfer of pollen from a male to a female part of the same or a different flower.

Pollinium (plural, *pollinia*): The pollen-bearing part of a flower.

Propagate: To cause to multiply.

Prothalium (plural, *prothalia*): The small green, scale-like sexual stage in the life-cycle of a fern.

Pubescent: Covered with down, or fine short hair.

Reaction: With reference to soils—degree of acidity or alkalinity; the pH number.

Rootball: Mass of earth surrounding the roots of plants when lifted for transplanting.

Rootstock: A wholly or partly subterranean stem (*not* root).

[206]

Sepals: The outer floral leaves which enter into a flower.

Sessile: Without a stalk or stem.

Shade-house: A building with semi-open roof and sides sheltering beds intended for growing shade-loving plants.

Sorus (plural, *sori*): A fruit-dot (*see above*).

Species: As used herein—a group of plants so nearly alike in their characteristics that they might all have come from a single parent.

Sphagnum bog: A swamp or bog in which sphagnum moss is the principal vegetation.

Sphagnum moss: A living moss-like plant found in northern bogs throughout the world.

Sporophyl: Fertile frond, bearing fruit-dots.

Subsoil: The layer of earth immediately under the surface soil.

Tap-root: A main root, penetrating deeply downward.

Topography: The 'lay of the land'—its ups and downs, ledges, and other surface characteristics.

Twice-pinnate: With pinnae again divided into 'pinnules.'

Bibliography

BOOKS QUOTED

Clute, Willard Nelson, *Our Ferns,* Philadelphia, 1938.
House, Homer D., *Wild Flowers of New York,* vols. I and II, Albany, 1923.
Moldenke, Harold N., *American Wildflowers,* New York and Toronto, 1949.
Wherry, Edgar T., *Wild Flower Guide,* New York, 1948.

RECOMMENDED READING

Bailey, L. H. and Ethel Zoe, *Hortus Second,* New York and Toronto, 1945.
Durand, Herbert, *Field Book of Common Ferns,* New York, 1928.
Gray's New Manual of Botany, 8th edition, New York, Cincinnati, and Chicago, 1950.
Hottes, Alfred Carl, *How To Increase Plants,* New York, 1949; *Plant Propagation,* New York, 1940.
Lutz, Harold J., and Chandler, Robert F., Jr., *Forest Soils,* New York, 1946.
Seymour, E. L. D. (ed.), *The Garden Encyclopedia,* New York, 1936.
Standardized Plant Names, 2nd edition, prepared for the American Joint Committee on Horticultural Nomenclature, by Harlan P. Kelsey and William A. Dayton, Harrisburg, Pa., 1942.
Wherry, Edgar T., *Guide to Eastern Ferns,* Lancaster, Pa., 1937.

Index

[211]

[212]

[215]

[216]

Maples, for compost, 11: pH of, 3, 11; for shade, 19; as winter-cover, 35
Marble, 18, 20
Marginal woodfern, 165–6
Markers, see Labels
Marshfern, 170–71
Marsh-marigold, common, 103
Mayapple, 107–8
Mayflower, 139–40
Meadow anemone, 101–2
Meadow-beauty, common, 130–31
Meal, castorbean, 11, 13, 18
Meal, cottonseed, 11–13, 18
Medeola virginiana, 75–6
Merrybells, big, 63
Merrybells, little, 62–3
Mertensia virginica, 146–7
Metal bands, 18–19, 34, 39
Metal foil, 53
Miami mist, 145–6
Mice, 33–4, 53
Microbes, see Micro-organisms
Micro-organisms, affected by pH, 5; in compost, 10, 12, 30; functions, 7, 30; moisture requirements, 30
Mitchella repens, 151–2
Mitella diphylla, 118
Miterwort, 117
Miterwort, false, 117
Moccasinflower, pink, 81–4
Moisture, see Humidity, Water, Watering
Moldenke, Harold N., quoted, 82–3, 88, 97
Molds, see Micro-organisms
Moles, 33–4
Monarda didyma, 146–7
Monotropa uniflora, 136–7
Monument-plant, 142–3
Morning glory, 40
Mosses, 15–16
Mountain aster, 155
  hollyfern, 180–81
  laurel, 138–9
  woodfern, 167–8
Mountain-fringe, 111–12
Mulch, see Groundlitter, Winter-cover
Muskrats, 33

Narrow beechfern, 161–2
Narrow swampfern, 163–4

Narrow-leaf spleenwort, 178–9
Narrow-leaved spring beauty, 98–9
Needlemold, collecting, 23, 26; on forest floor, 3; in gardens, 32; pH of, 8, 11, 33
Needles (of conifers), on forest floor, 3–4; on paths, 39; pH of, 6, 11, 19
New Jersey tea, 124–5
New York fern, 169–70
Nitrogen, 7, 30, 33
Nodding trillium, 78–9
Nodes, 46
Northern bedstraw, 151
Northern maidenhair fern, 171–2
Nothoscordum bivalve, 64
Nurserymen, 14, 17, 19–20, 23

Oak forest, 3
Oakfern, 16, 162–3
Oakleech, 148–9
Oaks, in forests, 3; micro-organisms in leaves, 12; pH of, 6, 11; for shade, 19–20; as wintercover, 35–6
Obolaria virginica, 143–4
Ocean spray, 19
Onoclea sensibilis, 186–7
Orangecup lily, 65
Orange-root, 107
Orange seeds, 40
Orchid, see also Orchis and Pogonia
  ciliaris, 89–90
  cranefly, 95–6
  family, 81–96
  fiveleaf, 91–2
  Hooker, 89–90
  little-bird, 90–91
  padleaf, 90
  puttyroot, 95
  roundleaf, 89
  satyr, 89
  seeds, 81
  white-fringe, 89
  yellow-fringe, 90–91
Orchidaceae, 81
Orchids, 7, 81
Orchis, showy, 87–8
  spectabilis, 87–8
  see also Orchid
Organic matter, in forests, 4; in compost, 10–14
Osmunda cinnamomea, 190–91
  claytoniana, 191

A CATALOGUE OF SELECTED DOVER BOOKS
IN ALL FIELDS OF INTEREST

A CATALOG OF SELECTED DOVER
BOOKS IN ALL FIELDS OF INTEREST

THE ART NOUVEAU STYLE, edited by Roberta Waddell. 579 rare photographs of works in jewelry, metalwork, glass, ceramics, textiles, architecture and furniture by 175 artists—Mucha, Seguy, Lalique, Tiffany, many others. 288pp. 8⅜ × 11¼.
23515-7 Pa. $8.95

AMERICAN COUNTRY HOUSES OF THE GILDED AGE (Sheldon's "Artistic Country-Seats"), A. Lewis. All of Sheldon's fascinating and historically important photographs and plans. New text by Arnold Lewis. Approx. 200 illustrations. 128pp. 9⅜ × 12¼.
24301-X Pa. $7.95

THE WAY WE LIVE NOW, Anthony Trollope. Trollope's late masterpiece, marks shift to bitter satire. Character Melmotte "his greatest villain." Reproduced from original edition with 40 illustrations. 416pp. 6⅛ × 9¼.
24360-5 Pa. $7.95

BENCHLEY LOST AND FOUND, Robert Benchley. Finest humor from early 30's, about pet peeves, child psychologists, post office and others. Mostly unavailable elsewhere. 73 illustrations by Peter Arno and others. 183pp. 5⅜ × 8½.
22410-4 Pa. $3.50

ISOMETRIC PERSPECTIVE DESIGNS AND HOW TO CREATE THEM, John Locke. Isometric perspective is the picture of an object adrift in imaginary space. 75 mindboggling designs. 52pp. 8¼ × 11.
24123-8 Pa. $2.50

PERSPECTIVE FOR ARTISTS, Rex Vicat Cole. Depth, perspective of sky and sea, shadows, much more, not usually covered. 391 diagrams, 81 reproductions of drawings and paintings. 279pp. 5⅜ × 8½.
22487-2 Pa. $4.00

MOVIE-STAR PORTRAITS OF THE FORTIES, edited by John Kobal. 163 glamor, studio photos of 106 stars of the 1940s: Rita Hayworth, Ava Gardner, Marlon Brando, Clark Gable, many more. 176pp. 8⅜ × 11¼.
23546-7 Pa. $6.95

STARS OF THE BROADWAY STAGE, 1940-1967, Fred Fehl. Marlon Brando, Uta Hagen, John Kerr, John Gielgud, Jessica Tandy in great shows—South Pacific, Galileo, West Side Story, more. 240 black-and-white photos. 144pp. 8⅜ × 11¼.
24398-2 Pa. $8.95

ILLUSTRATED DICTIONARY OF HISTORIC ARCHITECTURE, edited by Cyril M. Harris. Extraordinary compendium of clear, concise definitions for over 5000 important architectural terms complemented by over 2000 line drawings. 592pp. 7½ × 9⅜.
24444-X Pa. $14.95

THE EARLY WORK OF FRANK LLOYD WRIGHT, F.L. Wright. 207 rare photos of Oak Park period, first great buildings: Unity Temple, Dana house, Larkin factory. Complete photos of Wasmuth edition. New Introduction. 160pp. 8⅜ × 11¼.
24381-8 Pa. $7.50

LIVING MY LIFE, Emma Goldman. Candid, no holds barred account by foremost American anarchist: her own life, anarchist movement, famous contemporaries, ideas and their impact. 944pp. 5⅜ × 8½. 22543-7, 22544-5 Pa., Two-vol. set $13.00

UNDERSTANDING THERMODYNAMICS, H.C. Van Ness. Clear, lucid treatment of first and second laws of thermodynamics. Excellent supplement to basic textbook in undergraduate science or engineering class. 103pp. 5⅜ × 8.
63277-6 Pa. $3.50

25 KITES THAT FLY, Leslie Hunt. Full, easy-to-follow instructions for kites made from inexpensive materials. Many novelties. 70 illustrations. 110pp. 5⅜ × 8½.
22550-X Pa. $1.95

PIANO TUNING, J. Cree Fischer. Clearest, best book for beginner, amateur. Simple repairs, raising dropped notes, tuning by easy method of flattened fifths. No previous skills needed. 4 illustrations. 201pp. 5⅜ × 8½.
23267-0 Pa. $3.50

EARLY AMERICAN IRON-ON TRANSFER PATTERNS, edited by Rita Weiss. 75 designs, borders, alphabets, from traditional American sources. 48pp. 8¼ × 11.
23162-3 Pa. $1.95

CROCHETING EDGINGS, edited by Rita Weiss. Over 100 of the best designs for these lovely trims for a host of household items. Complete instructions, illustrations. 48pp. 8¼ × 11.
24031-2 Pa. $2.00

FINGER PLAYS FOR NURSERY AND KINDERGARTEN, Emilie Poulsson. 18 finger plays with music (voice and piano); entertaining, instructive. Counting, nature lore, etc. Victorian classic. 53 illustrations. 80pp. 6½ × 9¼. 22588-7 Pa. $1.95

BOSTON THEN AND NOW, Peter Vanderwarker. Here in 59 side-by-side views are photographic documentations of the city's past and present. 119 photographs. Full captions. 122pp. 8¼ × 11.
24312-5 Pa. $6.95

CROCHETING BEDSPREADS, edited by Rita Weiss. 22 patterns, originally published in three instruction books 1939-41. 39 photos, 8 charts. Instructions. 48pp. 8¼ × 11.
23610-2 Pa. $2.00

HAWTHORNE ON PAINTING, Charles W. Hawthorne. Collected from notes taken by students at famous Cape Cod School; hundreds of direct, personal *apercus*, ideas, suggestions. 91pp. 5⅜ × 8½.
20653-X Pa. $2.50

THERMODYNAMICS, Enrico Fermi. A classic of modern science. Clear, organized treatment of systems, first and second laws, entropy, thermodynamic potentials, etc. Calculus required. 160pp. 5⅜ × 8½.
60361-X Pa. $4.00

TEN BOOKS ON ARCHITECTURE, Vitruvius. The most important book ever written on architecture. Early Roman aesthetics, technology, classical orders, site selection, all other aspects. Morgan translation. 331pp. 5⅜ × 8½. 20645-9 Pa. $5.50

THE CORNELL BREAD BOOK, Clive M. McCay and Jeanette B. McCay. Famed high-protein recipe incorporated into breads, rolls, buns, coffee cakes, pizza, pie crusts, more. Nearly 50 illustrations. 48pp. 8¼ × 11.
23995-0 Pa. $2.00

THE CRAFTSMAN'S HANDBOOK, Cennino Cennini. 15th-century handbook, school of Giotto, explains applying gold, silver leaf; gesso; fresco painting, grinding pigments, etc. 142pp. 6⅛ × 9¼.
20054-X Pa. $3.50

FRANK LLOYD WRIGHT'S FALLINGWATER, Donald Hoffmann. Full story of Wright's masterwork at Bear Run, Pa. 100 photographs of site, construction, and details of completed structure. 112pp. 9¼ × 10.
23671-4 Pa. $6.50

OVAL STAINED GLASS PATTERN BOOK, C. Eaton. 60 new designs framed in shape of an oval. Greater complexity, challenge with sinuous cats, birds, mandalas framed in antique shape. 64pp. 8¼ × 11.
24519-5 Pa. $3.50

YUCATAN BEFORE AND AFTER THE CONQUEST, Diego de Landa. Only significant account of Yucatan written in the early post-Conquest era. Translated by William Gates. Over 120 illustrations. 162pp. 5⅜ × 8½. 23622-6 Pa. $3.50

ORNATE PICTORIAL CALLIGRAPHY, E.A. Lupfer. Complete instructions, over 150 examples help you create magnificent "flourishes" from which beautiful animals and objects gracefully emerge. 8⅛ × 11. 21957-7 Pa. $2.95

DOLLY DINGLE PAPER DOLLS, Grace Drayton. Cute chubby children by same artist who did Campbell Kids. Rare plates from 1910s. 30 paper dolls and over 100 outfits reproduced in full color. 32pp. 9¼ × 12¼. 23711-7 Pa. $2.95

CURIOUS GEORGE PAPER DOLLS IN FULL COLOR, H. A. Rey, Kathy Allert. Naughty little monkey-hero of children's books in two doll figures, plus 48 full-color costumes: pirate, Indian chief, fireman, more. 32pp. 9¼ × 12¼. 24386-9 Pa. $3.50

GERMAN: HOW TO SPEAK AND WRITE IT, Joseph Rosenberg. Like *French, How to Speak and Write It*. Very rich modern course, with a wealth of pictorial material. 330 illustrations. 384pp. 5⅜ × 8½. (USUKO) 20271-2 Pa. $4.75

CATS AND KITTENS: 24 Ready-to-Mail Color Photo Postcards, D. Holby. Handsome collection; feline in a variety of adorable poses. Identifications. 12pp. on postcard stock. 8¼ × 11. 24469-5 Pa. $2.95

MARILYN MONROE PAPER DOLLS, Tom Tierney. 31 full-color designs on heavy stock, from *The Asphalt Jungle, Gentlemen Prefer Blondes*, 22 others. 1 doll. 16 plates. 32pp. 9⅜ × 12¼. 23769-9 Pa. $3.50

FUNDAMENTALS OF LAYOUT, F.H. Wills. All phases of layout design discussed and illustrated in 121 illustrations. Indispensable as student's text or handbook for professional. 124pp. 8⅛.× 11. 21279-3 Pa. $4.50

FANTASTIC SUPER STICKERS, Ed Sibbett, Jr. 75 colorful pressure-sensitive stickers. Peel off and place for a touch of pizzazz: clowns, penguins, teddy bears, etc. Full color. 16pp. 8¼ × 11. 24471-7 Pa. $2.95

LABELS FOR ALL OCCASIONS, Ed Sibbett, Jr. 6 labels each of 16 different designs—baroque, art nouveau, art deco, Pennsylvania Dutch, etc.—in full color. 24pp. 8¼ × 11. 23688-9 Pa. $2.95

HOW TO CALCULATE QUICKLY: RAPID METHODS IN BASIC MATHE-MATICS, Henry Sticker. Addition, subtraction, multiplication, division, checks, etc. More than 8000 problems, solutions. 185pp. 5 × 7¼. 20295-X Pa. $2.95

THE CAT COLORING BOOK, Karen Baldauski. Handsome, realistic renderings of 40 splendid felines, from American shorthair to exotic types. 44 plates. Captions. 48pp. 8¼ × 11. 24011-8 Pa. $2.25

THE TALE OF PETER RABBIT, Beatrix Potter. The inimitable Peter's terrifying adventure in Mr. McGregor's garden, with all 27 wonderful, full-color Potter illustrations. 55pp. 4¼ × 5½. (Available in U.S. only) 22827-4 Pa. $1.50

BASIC ELECTRICITY, U.S. Bureau of Naval Personnel. Batteries, circuits, conductors, AC and DC, inductance and capacitance, generators, motors, trans-formers, amplifiers, etc. 349 illustrations. 448pp. 6½ × 9¼. 20973-3 Pa. $7.95

SMOCKING: TECHNIQUE, PROJECTS, AND DESIGNS, Dianne Durand. Foremost smocking designer provides complete instructions on how to smock. Over 10 projects, over 100 illustrations. 56pp. 8¼ × 11. 23788-5 Pa. $2.00

AUDUBON'S BIRDS IN COLOR FOR DECOUPAGE, edited by Eleanor H. Rawlings. 24 sheets, 37 most decorative birds, full color, on one side of paper. Instructions, including work under glass. 56pp. 8¼ × 11. 23492-4 Pa. $3.50

THE COMPLETE BOOK OF SILK SCREEN PRINTING PRODUCTION, J.I. Biegeleisen. For commercial user, teacher in advanced classes, serious hobbyist. Most modern techniques, materials, equipment for optimal results. 124 illustrations. 253pp. 5⅝ × 8½. 21100-2 Pa. $4.50

A TREASURY OF ART NOUVEAU DESIGN AND ORNAMENT, edited by Carol Belanger Grafton. 577 designs for the practicing artist. Full-page, spots, borders, bookplates by Klimt, Bradley, others. 144pp. 8⅜ × 11¼. 24001-0 Pa. $5.00

ART NOUVEAU TYPOGRAPHIC ORNAMENTS, Dan X. Solo. Over 800 Art Nouveau florals, swirls, women, animals, borders, scrolls, wreaths, spots and dingbats, copyright-free. 100pp. 8⅛ × 11. 24366-4 Pa. $4.00

HAND SHADOWS TO BE THROWN UPON THE WALL, Henry Bursill. Wonderful Victorian novelty tells how to make flying birds, dog, goose, deer, and 14 others, each explained by a full-page illustration. 32pp. 6½ × 9¼. 21779-5 Pa. $1.50

AUDUBON'S BIRDS OF AMERICA COLORING BOOK, John James Audubon. Rendered for coloring by Paul Kennedy. 46 of Audubon's noted illustrations: red-winged black-bird, cardinal, etc. Original plates reproduced in full-color on the covers. Captions. 48pp. 8¼ × 11. 23049-X Pa. $2.25

SILK SCREEN TECHNIQUES, J.I. Biegeleisen, M.A. Cohn. Clear, practical, modern, economical. Minimal equipment (self-built), materials, easy methods. For amateur, hobbyist, 1st book. 141 illustrations. 185pp. 6⅛ × 9¼. 20433-2 Pa. $3.95

101 PATCHWORK PATTERNS, Ruby S. McKim. 101 beautiful, immediately useable patterns, full-size, modern and traditional. Also general information, estimating, quilt lore. 140 illustrations. 124pp. 7⅞ × 10¾. 20773-0 Pa. $3.50

READY-TO-USE FLORAL DESIGNS, Ed Sibbett, Jr. Over 100 floral designs (most in three sizes) of popular individual blossoms as well as bouquets, sprays, garlands. 64pp. 8¼ × 11. 23976-4 Pa. $2.95

AMERICAN WILD FLOWERS COLORING BOOK, Paul Kennedy. Planned coverage of 46 most important wildflowers, from Rickett's collection; instructive as well as entertaining. Color versions on covers. Captions. 48pp. 8¼ × 11. 20095-7 Pa. $2.25

CARVING DUCK DECOYS, Harry V. Shourds and Anthony Hillman. Detailed instructions and full-size templates for constructing 16 beautiful, marvelously practical decoys according to time-honored South Jersey method. 70pp. 9¼ × 12¼. 24083-5 Pa. $4.95

TRADITIONAL PATCHWORK PATTERNS, Carol Belanger Grafton. Cardboard cut-out pieces for use as templates to make 12 quilts: Buttercup, Ribbon Border, Tree of Paradise, nine more. Full instructions. 57pp. 8¼ × 11. 23015-5 Pa. $3.50

TOLL HOUSE TRIED AND TRUE RECIPES, Ruth Graves Wakefield. Popovers, veal and ham loaf, baked beans, much more from the famous Mass. restaurant. Nearly 700 recipes. 376pp. 5⅜ × 8½. 23560-2 Pa. $4.95

FAVORITE CHRISTMAS CAROLS, selected and arranged by Charles J.F. Cofone. Title, music, first verse and refrain of 34 traditional carols in handsome calligraphy; also subsequent verses and other information in type. 79pp. 8⅜ × 11. 20445-6 Pa. $3.00

CAMERA WORK: A PICTORIAL GUIDE, Alfred Stieglitz. All 559 illustrations from most important periodical in history of art photography. Reduced in size but still clear, in strict chronological order, with complete captions. 176pp. 8⅜ × 11¼. 23591-2 Pa. $6.95

FAVORITE SONGS OF THE NINETIES, edited by Robert Fremont. 88 favorites: "Ta-Ra-Ra-Boom-De-Aye," "The Band Played On," "Bird in a Gilded Cage," etc. 401pp. 9 × 12. 21536-9 Pa. $10.95

STRING FIGURES AND HOW TO MAKE THEM, Caroline F. Jayne. Fullest, clearest instructions on string figures from around world: Eskimo, Navajo, Lapp, Europe, more. Cat's cradle, moving spear, lightning, stars. 950 illustrations. 407pp. 5⅜ × 8½. 20152-X Pa. $4.95

LIFE IN ANCIENT EGYPT, Adolf Erman. Detailed older account, with much not in more recent books: domestic life, religion, magic, medicine, commerce, and whatever else needed for complete picture. Many illustrations. 597pp. 5⅜ × 8½. 22632-8 Pa. $7.95

ANCIENT EGYPT: ITS CULTURE AND HISTORY, J.E. Manchip White. From pre-dynastics through Ptolemies: scoiety, history, political structure, religion, daily life, literature, cultural heritage. 48 plates. 217pp. 5⅜ × 8½. (EBE) 22548-8 Pa. $4.95

KEPT IN THE DARK, Anthony Trollope. Unusual short novel about Victorian morality and abnormal psychology by the great English author. Probably the first American publication. Frontispiece by Sir John Millais. 92pp. 6½ × 9¼. 23609-9 Pa. $2.95

MAN AND WIFE, Wilkie Collins. Nineteenth-century master launches an attack on out-moded Scottish marital laws and Victorian cult of athleticism. Artfully plotted. 35 illustrations. 239pp. 6⅛ × 9¼. 24451-2 Pa. $5.95

RELATIVITY AND COMMON SENSE, Herman Bondi. Radically reoriented presentation of Einstein's Special Theory and one of most valuable popular accounts available. 60 illustrations. 177pp. 5⅜ × 8. (EUK) 24021-5 Pa. $3.50

THE EGYPTIAN BOOK OF THE DEAD, E.A. Wallis Budge. Complete reproduction of Ani's papyrus, finest ever found. Full hieroglyphic text, interlinear transliteration, word-for-word translation, smooth translation. 533pp. 6½ × 9¼. (USO) 21866-X Pa. $8.50

COUNTRY AND SUBURBAN HOMES OF THE PRAIRIE SCHOOL PERIOD, H.V. von Holst. Over 400 photographs floor plans, elevations, detailed drawings (exteriors and interiors) for over 100 structures. Text. Important primary source. 128pp. 8⅜ × 11¼. 24373-7 Pa. $5.95

CATALOG OF DOVER BOOKS

THE RIME OF THE ANCIENT MARINER, Gustave Doré, S.T. Coleridge. Doré's finest work, 34 plates capture moods, subtleties of poem. Full text. 77pp. 9¼ × 12. 22305-1 Pa. $4.95

SONGS OF INNOCENCE, William Blake. The first and most popular of Blake's famous "Illuminated Books," in a facsimile edition reproducing all 31 brightly colored plates. Additional printed text of each poem. 64pp. 5¼ × 7. 22764-2 Pa. $3.00

AN INTRODUCTION TO INFORMATION THEORY, J.R. Pierce. Second (1980) edition of most impressive non-technical account available. Encoding, entropy, noisy channel, related areas, etc. 320pp. 5⅜ × 8½. 24061-4 Pa. $4.95

THE DIVINE PROPORTION: A STUDY IN MATHEMATICAL BEAUTY, H.E. Huntley. "Divine proportion" or "golden ratio" in poetry, Pascal's triangle, philosophy, psychology, music, mathematical figures, etc. Excellent bridge between science and art. 58 figures. 185pp. 5⅜ × 8½. 22254-3 Pa. $3.95

THE DOVER NEW YORK WALKING GUIDE: From the Battery to Wall Street, Mary J. Shapiro. Superb inexpensive guide to historic buildings and locales in lower Manhattan: Trinity Church, Bowling Green, more. Complete Text; maps. 36 illustrations. 48pp. 3⅞ × 9¼. 24225-0 Pa. $1.75

NEW YORK THEN AND NOW, Edward B. Watson, Edmund V. Gillon, Jr. 83 important Manhattan sites: on facing pages early photographs (1875-1925) and 1976 photos by Gillon. 172 illustrations. 171pp. 9¼ × 10. 23361-8 Pa. $7.95

HISTORIC COSTUME IN PICTURES, Braun & Schneider. Over 1450 costumed figures from dawn of civilization to end of 19th century. English captions. 125 plates. 256pp. 8⅜ × 11¼. 23150-X Pa. $7.50

VICTORIAN AND EDWARDIAN FASHION: A Photographic Survey, Alison Gernsheim. First fashion history completely illustrated by contemporary photographs. Full text plus 235 photos, 1840-1914, in which many celebrities appear. 240pp. 6½ × 9¼. 24205-6 Pa. $6.00

CHARTED CHRISTMAS DESIGNS FOR COUNTED CROSS-STITCH AND OTHER NEEDLECRAFTS, Lindberg Press. Charted designs for 45 beautiful needlecraft projects with many yuletide and wintertime motifs. 48pp. 8¼ × 11. 24356-7 Pa. $1.95

101 FOLK DESIGNS FOR COUNTED CROSS-STITCH AND OTHER NEEDLE-CRAFTS, Carter Houck. 101 authentic charted folk designs in a wide array of lovely representations with many suggestions for effective use. 48pp. 8¼ × 11. 24369-9 Pa. $1.95

FIVE ACRES AND INDEPENDENCE, Maurice G. Kains. Great back-to-the-land classic explains basics of self-sufficient farming. The one book to get. 95 illustrations. 397pp. 5⅜ × 8½. 20974-1 Pa. $4.95

A MODERN HERBAL, Margaret Grieve. Much the fullest, most exact, most useful compilation of herbal material. Gigantic alphabetical encyclopedia, from aconite to zedoary, gives botanical information, medical properties, folklore, economic uses, and much else. Indispensable to serious reader. 161 illustrations. 888pp. 6½ × 9¼. (Available in U.S. only) 22798-7, 22799-5 Pa., Two-vol. set $16.45

HOW THE OTHER HALF LIVES, Jacob A. Riis. Journalistic record of filth, degradation, upward drive in New York immigrant slums, shops, around 1900. New edition includes 100 original Riis photos, monuments of early photography. 233pp. 10 × 7⅞. 22012-5 Pa. $7.95

CHINA AND ITS PEOPLE IN EARLY PHOTOGRAPHS, John Thomson. In 200 black-and-white photographs of exceptional quality photographic pioneer Thomson captures the mountains, dwellings, monuments and people of 19th-century China. 272pp. 9⅜ × 12¼. 24393-1 Pa. $12.95

GODEY COSTUME PLATES IN COLOR FOR DECOUPAGE AND FRAMING, edited by Eleanor Hasbrouk Rawlings. 24 full-color engravings depicting 19th-century Parisian haute couture. Printed on one side only. 56pp. 8¼ × 11. 23879-2 Pa. $3.95

ART NOUVEAU STAINED GLASS PATTERN BOOK, Ed Sibbett, Jr. 104 projects using well-known themes of Art Nouveau: swirling forms, florals, peacocks, and sensuous women. 60pp. 8¼ × 11. 23577-7 Pa. $3.00

QUICK AND EASY PATCHWORK ON THE SEWING MACHINE: Susan Aylsworth Murwin and Suzzy Payne. Instructions, diagrams show exactly how to machine sew 12 quilts. 48pp. of templates. 50 figures. 80pp. 8¼ × 11. 23770-2 Pa. $3.50

THE STANDARD BOOK OF QUILT MAKING AND COLLECTING, Marguerite Ickis. Full information, full-sized patterns for making 46 traditional quilts, also 150 other patterns. 483 illustrations. 273pp. 6⅞ × 9⅝. 20582-7 Pa. $5.95

LETTERING AND ALPHABETS, J. Albert Cavanagh. 85 complete alphabets lettered in various styles; instructions for spacing, roughs, brushwork. 121pp. 8¾ × 8. 20053-1 Pa. $3.75

LETTER FORMS: 110 COMPLETE ALPHABETS, Frederick Lambert. 110 sets of capital letters; 16 lower case alphabets; 70 sets of numbers and other symbols. 110pp. 8⅛ × 11. 22872-X Pa. $4.50

ORCHIDS AS HOUSE PLANTS, Rebecca Tyson Northen. Grow cattleyas and many other kinds of orchids—in a window, in a case, or under artificial light. 63 illustrations. 148pp. 5⅜ × 8½. 23261-1 Pa. $2.95

THE MUSHROOM HANDBOOK, Louis C.C. Krieger. Still the best popular handbook. Full descriptions of 259 species, extremely thorough text, poisons, folklore, etc. 32 color plates; 126 other illustrations. 560pp. 5⅜ × 8½. 21861-9 Pa. $8.50

THE DORÉ BIBLE ILLUSTRATIONS, Gustave Doré. All wonderful, detailed plates: Adam and Eve, Flood, Babylon, life of Jesus, etc. Brief King James text with each plate. 241 plates. 241pp. 9 × 12. 23004-X Pa. $6.95

THE BOOK OF KELLS: Selected Plates in Full Color, edited by Blanche Cirker. 32 full-page plates from greatest manuscript-icon of early Middle Ages. Fantastic, mysterious. Publisher's Note. Captions. 32pp. 9⅜ × 12¼. 24345-1 Pa. $4.50

THE PERFECT WAGNERITE, George Bernard Shaw. Brilliant criticism of the Ring Cycle, with provocative interpretation of politics, economic theories behind the Ring. 136pp. 5⅜ × 8½. (Available in U.S. only) 21707-8 Pa. $3.00

CATALOG OF DOVER BOOKS

DECORATIVE NAPKIN FOLDING FOR BEGINNERS, Lillian Oppenheimer and Natalie Epstein. 22 different napkin folds in the shape of a heart, clown's hat, love knot, etc. 63 drawings. 48pp. 8¼ × 11. 23797-4 Pa. $1.95

DECORATIVE LABELS FOR HOME CANNING, PRESERVING, AND OTHER HOUSEHOLD AND GIFT USES, Theodore Menten. 128 gummed, perforated labels, beautifully printed in 2 colors. 12 versions. Adhere to metal, glass, wood, ceramics. 24pp. 8¼ × 11. 23219-0 Pa. $2.95

EARLY AMERICAN STENCILS ON WALLS AND FURNITURE, Janet Waring. Thorough coverage of 19th-century folk art: techniques, artifacts, surviving specimens. 166 illustrations, 7 in color. 147pp. of text. 7⅞ × 10¾. 21906-2 Pa. $8.95

AMERICAN ANTIQUE WEATHERVANES, A.B. & W.T. Westervelt. Extensively illustrated 1883 catalog exhibiting over 550 copper weathervanes and finials. Excellent primary source by one of the principal manufacturers. 104pp. 6⅛ × 9¼. 24396-6 Pa. $3.95

ART STUDENTS' ANATOMY, Edmond J. Farris. Long favorite in art schools. Basic elements, common positions, actions. Full text, 158 illustrations. 159pp. 5⅜ × 8½. 20744-7 Pa. $3.50

BRIDGMAN'S LIFE DRAWING, George B. Bridgman. More than 500 drawings and text teach you to abstract the body into its major masses. Also specific areas of anatomy. 192pp. 6½ × 9¼. (EA) 22710-3 Pa. $4.50

COMPLETE PRELUDES AND ETUDES FOR SOLO PIANO, Frederic Chopin. All 26 Preludes, all 27 Etudes by greatest composer of piano music. Authoritative Paderewski edition. 224pp. 9 × 12. (Available in U.S. only) 24052-5 Pa. $6.95

PIANO MUSIC 1888-1905, Claude Debussy. Deux Arabesques, Suite Bergamesque, Masques, 1st series of Images, etc. 9 others, in corrected editions. 175pp. 9⅜ × 12¼. (ECE) 22771-5 Pa. $5.95

TEDDY BEAR IRON-ON TRANSFER PATTERNS, Ted Menten. 80 iron-on transfer patterns of male and female Teddys in a wide variety of activities, poses, sizes. 48pp. 8¼ × 11. 24596-9 Pa. $2.00

A PICTURE HISTORY OF THE BROOKLYN BRIDGE, M.J. Shapiro. Profusely illustrated account of greatest engineering achievement of 19th century. 167 rare photos & engravings recall construction, human drama. Extensive, detailed text. 122pp. 8¼ × 11. 24403-2 Pa. $7.95

NEW YORK IN THE THIRTIES, Berenice Abbott. Noted photographer's fascinating study shows new buildings that have become famous and old sights that have disappeared forever. 97 photographs. 97pp. 11⅜ × 10. 22967-X Pa. $6.50

MATHEMATICAL TABLES AND FORMULAS, Robert D. Carmichael and Edwin R. Smith. Logarithms, sines, tangents, trig functions, powers, roots, reciprocals, exponential and hyperbolic functions, formulas and theorems. 269pp. 5⅜ × 8½. 60111-0 Pa. $3.75

HANDBOOK OF MATHEMATICAL FUNCTIONS WITH FORMULAS, GRAPHS, AND MATHEMATICAL TABLES, edited by Milton Abramowitz and Irene A. Stegun. Vast compendium: 29 sets of tables, some to as high as 20 places. 1,046pp. 8 × 10½. 61272-4 Pa. $19.95

KEYBOARD WORKS FOR SOLO INSTRUMENTS, G.F. Handel. 35 neglected works from Handel's vast oeuvre, originally jotted down as improvisations. Includes Eight Great Suites, others. New sequence. 174pp. 9⅜ × 12¼.
24338-9 Pa. $7.50

AMERICAN LEAGUE BASEBALL CARD CLASSICS, Bert Randolph Sugar. 82 stars from 1900s to 60s on facsimile cards. Ruth, Cobb, Mantle, Williams, plus advertising, info, no duplications. Perforated, detachable. 16pp. 8¼ × 11.
24286-2 Pa. $2.95

A TREASURY OF CHARTED DESIGNS FOR NEEDLEWORKERS, Georgia Gorham and Jeanne Warth. 141 charted designs: owl, cat with yarn, tulips, piano, spinning wheel, covered bridge, Victorian house and many others. 48pp. 8¼ × 11.
23558-0 Pa. $1.95

DANISH FLORAL CHARTED DESIGNS, Gerda Bengtsson. Exquisite collection of over 40 different florals: anemone, Iceland poppy, wild fruit, pansies, many others. 45 illustrations. 48pp. 8¼ × 11. 23957-8 Pa. $1.75

OLD PHILADELPHIA IN EARLY PHOTOGRAPHS 1839-1914, Robert F. Looney. 215 photographs: panoramas, street scenes, landmarks, President-elect Lincoln's visit, 1876 Centennial Exposition, much more. 230pp. 8⅜ × 11¾.
23345-6 Pa. $9.95

PRELUDE TO MATHEMATICS, W.W. Sawyer. Noted mathematician's lively, stimulating account of non-Euclidean geometry, matrices, determinants, group theory, other topics. Emphasis on novel, striking aspects. 224pp. 5⅜ × 8½.
24401-6 Pa. $4.50

ADVENTURES WITH A MICROSCOPE, Richard Headstrom. 59 adventures with clothing fibers, protozoa, ferns and lichens, roots and leaves, much more. 142 illustrations. 232pp. 5⅜ × 8½. 23471-1 Pa. $3.50

IDENTIFYING ANIMAL TRACKS: MAMMALS, BIRDS, AND OTHER ANIMALS OF THE EASTERN UNITED STATES, Richard Headstrom. For hunters, naturalists, scouts, nature-lovers. Diagrams of tracks, tips on identification. 128pp. 5⅜ × 8. 24442-3 Pa. $3.50

VICTORIAN FASHIONS AND COSTUMES FROM HARPER'S BAZAR, 1867-1898, edited by Stella Blum. Day costumes, evening wear, sports clothes, shoes, hats, other accessories in over 1,000 detailed engravings. 320pp. 9⅜ × 12¼.
22990-4 Pa. $9.95

EVERYDAY FASHIONS OF THE TWENTIES AS PICTURED IN SEARS AND OTHER CATALOGS, edited by Stella Blum. Actual dress of the Roaring Twenties, with text by Stella Blum. Over 750 illustrations, captions. 156pp. 9 × 12.
24134-3 Pa. $7.95

HALL OF FAME BASEBALL CARDS, edited by Bert Randolph Sugar. Cy Young, Ted Williams, Lou Gehrig, and many other Hall of Fame greats on 92 full-color, detachable reprints of early baseball cards. No duplication of cards with *Classic Baseball Cards*. 16pp. 8¼ × 11. 23624-2 Pa. $2.95

THE ART OF HAND LETTERING, Helm Wotzkow. Course in hand lettering, Roman, Gothic, Italic, Block, Script. Tools, proportions, optical aspects, individual variation. Very quality conscious. Hundreds of specimens. 320pp. 5⅜ × 8½.
21797-3 Pa. $4.95

CATALOG OF DOVER BOOKS

TWENTY-FOUR ART NOUVEAU POSTCARDS IN FULL COLOR FROM CLASSIC POSTERS, Hayward and Blanche Cirker. Ready-to-mail postcards reproduced from rare set of poster art. Works by Toulouse-Lautrec, Parrish, Steinlen, Mucha, Cheret, others. 12pp. 8¼× 11. 24389-3 Pa. $2.95

READY-TO-USE ART NOUVEAU BOOKMARKS IN FULL COLOR, Carol Belanger Grafton. 30 elegant bookmarks featuring graceful, flowing lines, foliate motifs, sensuous women characteristic of Art Nouveau. Perforated for easy detaching. 16pp. 8¼ × 11. 24305-2 Pa. $2.95

FRUIT KEY AND TWIG KEY TO TREES AND SHRUBS, William M. Harlow. Fruit key covers 120 deciduous and evergreen species; twig key covers 160 deciduous species. Easily used. Over 300 photographs. 126pp. 5⅜ × 8½. 20511-8 Pa. $2.25

LEONARDO DRAWINGS, Leonardo da Vinci. Plants, landscapes, human face and figure, etc., plus studies for Sforza monument, *Last Supper*, more. 60 illustrations. 64pp. 8¼ × 11⅛. 23951-9 Pa. $2.75

CLASSIC BASEBALL CARDS, edited by Bert R. Sugar. 98 classic cards on heavy stock, full color, perforated for detaching. Ruth, Cobb, Durocher, DiMaggio, H. Wagner, 99 others. Rare originals cost hundreds. 16pp. 8¼ × 11. 23498-3 Pa. $2.95

TREES OF THE EASTERN AND CENTRAL UNITED STATES AND CANADA, William M. Harlow. Best one-volume guide to 140 trees. Full descriptions, woodlore, range, etc. Over 600 illustrations. Handy size. 288pp. 4½ × 6⅜. 20395-6 Pa. $3.50

JUDY GARLAND PAPER DOLLS IN FULL COLOR, Tom Tierney. 3 Judy Garland paper dolls (teenager, grown-up, and mature woman) and 30 gorgeous costumes highlighting memorable career. Captions. 32pp. 9¼ × 12¼. 24404-0 Pa. $3.50

GREAT FASHION DESIGNS OF THE BELLE EPOQUE PAPER DOLLS IN FULL COLOR, Tom Tierney. Two dolls and 30 costumes meticulously rendered. Haute couture by Worth, Lanvin, Paquin, other greats late Victorian to WWI. 32pp. 9¼ × 12¼. 24425-3 Pa. $3.50

FASHION PAPER DOLLS FROM GODEY'S LADY'S BOOK, 1840-1854, Susan Johnston. In full color: 7 female fashion dolls with 50 costumes. Little girl's, bridal, riding, bathing, wedding, evening, everyday, etc. 32pp. 9¼ × 12¼. 23511-4 Pa. $3.50

THE BOOK OF THE SACRED MAGIC OF ABRAMELIN THE MAGE, translated by S. MacGregor Mathers. Medieval manuscript of ceremonial magic. Basic document in Aleister Crowley, Golden Dawn groups. 268pp. 5⅜ × 8½. 23211-5 Pa. $5.00

PETER RABBIT POSTCARDS IN FULL COLOR: 24 Ready-to-Mail Cards, Susan Whited LaBelle. Bunnies ice-skating, coloring Easter eggs, making valentines, many other charming scenes. 24 perforated full-color postcards, each measuring 4¼ × 6, on coated stock. 12pp. 9 × 12. 24617-5 Pa. $2.95

CELTIC HAND STROKE BY STROKE, A. Baker. Complete guide creating each letter of the alphabet in distinctive Celtic manner. Covers hand position, strokes, pens, inks, paper, more. Illustrated. 48pp. 8¼ × 11. 24336-2 Pa. $2.50

REASON IN ART, George Santayana. Renowned philosopher's provocative, seminal treatment of basis of art in instinct and experience. Volume Four of *The Life of Reason*. 230pp. 5⅜ × 8. 24358-3 Pa. $4.50

LANGUAGE, TRUTH AND LOGIC, Alfred J. Ayer. Famous, clear introduction to Vienna, Cambridge schools of Logical Positivism. Role of philosophy, elimination of metaphysics, nature of analysis, etc. 160pp. 5⅜ × 8½. (USCO) 20010-8 Pa. $2.75

BASIC ELECTRONICS, U.S. Bureau of Naval Personnel. Electron tubes, circuits, antennas, AM, FM, and CW transmission and receiving, etc. 560 illustrations. 567pp. 6½ × 9¼. 21076-6 Pa. $8.95

THE ART DECO STYLE, edited by Theodore Menten. Furniture, jewelry, metalwork, ceramics, fabrics, lighting fixtures, interior decors, exteriors, graphics from pure French sources. Over 400 photographs. 183pp. 8⅜ × 11¼. 22824-X Pa. $6.95

THE FOUR BOOKS OF ARCHITECTURE, Andrea Palladio. 16th-century classic covers classical architectural remains, Renaissance revivals, classical orders, etc. 1738 Ware English edition. 216 plates. 110pp. of text. 9½ × 12¾. 21308-0 Pa. $10.00

THE WIT AND HUMOR OF OSCAR WILDE, edited by Alvin Redman. More than 1000 ripostes, paradoxes, wisecracks: Work is the curse of the drinking classes, I can resist everything except temptations, etc. 258pp. 5⅜ × 8½. (USCO) 20602-5 Pa. $3.50

THE DEVIL'S DICTIONARY, Ambrose Bierce. Barbed, bitter, brilliant witticisms in the form of a dictionary. Best, most ferocious satire America has produced. 145pp. 5⅜ × 8½. 20487-1 Pa. $2.50

ERTÉ'S FASHION DESIGNS, Erté. 210 black-and-white inventions from *Harper's Bazar*, 1918-32, plus 8pp. full-color covers. Captions. 88pp. 9 × 12. 24203-X Pa. $6.50

ERTÉ GRAPHICS, Erté. Collection of striking color graphics: *Seasons, Alphabet, Numerals, Aces* and *Precious Stones*. 50 plates, including 4 on covers. 48pp. 9⅜ × 12¼. 23580-7 Pa. $6.95

PAPER FOLDING FOR BEGINNERS, William D. Murray and Francis J. Rigney. Clearest book for making origami sail boats, roosters, frogs that move legs, etc. 40 projects. More than 275 illustrations. 94pp. 5⅜ × 8½. 20713-7 Pa. $1.95

ORIGAMI FOR THE ENTHUSIAST, John Montroll. Fish, ostrich, peacock, squirrel, rhinoceros, Pegasus, 19 other intricate subjects. Instructions. Diagrams. 128pp. 9 × 12. 23799-0 Pa. $4.95

CROCHETING NOVELTY POT HOLDERS, edited by Linda Macho. 64 useful, whimsical pot holders feature kitchen themes, animals, flowers, other novelties. Surprisingly easy to crochet. Complete instructions. 48pp. 8¼ × 11. 24296-X Pa. $1.95

CROCHETING DOILIES, edited by Rita Weiss. Irish Crochet, Jewel, Star Wheel, Vanity Fair and more. Also luncheon and console sets, runners and centerpieces. 51 illustrations. 48pp. 8¼ × 11. 23424-X Pa. $2.00

READY-TO-USE BORDERS, Ted Menten. Both traditional and unusual interchangeable borders in a tremendous array of sizes, shapes, and styles. 32 plates. 64pp. 8¼ × 11. 23782-6 Pa. $2.95

THE WHOLE CRAFT OF SPINNING, Carol Kroll. Preparing fiber, drop spindle, treadle wheel, other fibers, more. Highly creative, yet simple. 43 illustrations. 48pp. 8¼ × 11. 23968-3 Pa. $2.50

HIDDEN PICTURE PUZZLE COLORING BOOK, Anna Pomaska. 31 delightful pictures to color with dozens of objects, people and animals hidden away to find. Captions. Solutions. 48pp. 8¼ × 11. 23909-8 Pa. $2.25

QUILTING WITH STRIPS AND STRINGS, H.W. Rose. Quickest, easiest way to turn left-over fabric into handsome quilt. 46 patchwork quilts; 31 full-size templates. 48pp. 8¼ × 11. 24357-5 Pa. $3.25

NATURAL DYES AND HOME DYEING, Rita J. Adrosko. Over 135 specific recipes from historical sources for cotton, wool, other fabrics. Genuine premodern handicrafts. 12 illustrations. 160pp. 5⅜ × 8½. 22688-3 Pa. $2.95

CARVING REALISTIC BIRDS, H.D. Green. Full-sized patterns, step-by-step instructions for robins, jays, cardinals, finches, etc. 97 illustrations. 80pp. 8¼ × 11. 23484-3 Pa. $3.00

GEOMETRY, RELATIVITY AND THE FOURTH DIMENSION, Rudolf Rucker. Exposition of fourth dimension, concepts of relativity as Flatland characters continue adventures. Popular, easily followed yet accurate, profound. 141 illustrations. 133pp. 5⅜ × 8½. 23400-2 Pa. $2.75

READY-TO-USE SMALL FRAMES AND BORDERS, Carol B. Grafton. Graphic message? Frame it graphically with 373 new frames and borders in many styles: Art Nouveau, Art Deco, Op Art. 64pp. 8¼ × 11. 24375-3 Pa. $2.95

CELTIC ART: THE METHODS OF CONSTRUCTION, George Bain. Simple geometric techniques for making Celtic interlacements, spirals, Kellstype initials, animals, humans, etc. Over 500 illustrations. 160pp. 9 × 12. (Available in U.S. only) 22923-8 Pa. $6.00

THE TALE OF TOM KITTEN, Beatrix Potter. Exciting text and all 27 vivid, full-color illustrations to charming tale of naughty little Tom getting into mischief again. 58pp. 4¼ × 5½. 24502-0 Pa. $1.50

WOODEN PUZZLE TOYS, Ed Sibbett, Jr. Transfer patterns and instructions for 24 easy-to-do projects: fish, butterflies, cats, acrobats, Humpty Dumpty, 19 others. 48pp. 8¼ × 11. 23713-3 Pa. $2.50

MY FAMILY TREE WORKBOOK, Rosemary A. Chorzempa. Enjoyable, easy-to-use introduction to genealogy designed specially for children. Data pages plus text. Instructive, educational, valuable. 64pp. 8¼ × 11. 24229-3 Pa. $2.25

Prices subject to change without notice.
Available at your book dealer or write for free catalog to Dept. GI, Dover Publications, Inc., 31 East 2nd St. Mineola, N.Y. 11501. Dover publishes more than 175 books each year on science, elementary and advanced mathematics, biology, music, art, literary history, social sciences and other areas.